I0820165

my southern kitchen

FROM SUPPERS TO CELEBRATIONS, RECIPES FOR EVERY OCCASION

Ivy Odom

Southern Living

Abrams, New York

Recipe Coco Cola Squares
from the kitchen of Grandmother Gladys
1 cup coke
2 cups plain flour
2 cups sugar
3 Tbsp. Hershey Cocoa
2 sticks oleo
1/2 cup buttermilk
2 beaten eggs
1 tsp. baking soda
1 1/2 cups mini marshmellows
1 tsp vanilla
Mix Sugar and Flour in bowl. Heat coke, oleo, and cocoa to boiling - add marsh-mellows and melt over low heat. Return mixture to boiling. Add to flour + Sugar mixture. Beat. Add beaten eggs
...and serve it with love.
over
Nana's Kitchen
Nana's Kitchen
Nana's Kitchen
Tea Cakes
400° cook appx. 10-15 minutes
3 1/2 cups all purpose flour
1 tsp salt
1 tsp baking powder
1 Tblsp vanilla
1 cup butter
2 eggs
2 cups sugar
Mix well -

my southern kitchen

contents

nana grandma kim bailey

aunt bean beth myriam margaret

aunt kirsten ginger aunt patti

mrs. wanda paige nicole kristin

donna rebecca lovett marsha sally

kari cara

For my Mama,
and all the strong Southern women
I get to call my family and friends.

amy janie

rebecca lang heather aunt brenda

shelbie kara jessica kristy

kathy megan lily anne connie

blakeslee dayna mama jane

dean fox lorna ronda palisa

con Chile
REFRESCO NATURAL
Creature Comforts
Brewing Co.
TROPICÁLIA
IPA

foreword

The first time Ivy Odom's talent caught my attention, she was an intern and fresh out of culinary school. One day I got word that a young test kitchen assistant was making a showstopping dessert I really needed to see. I went up upstairs to our food studios, the sprawling space where we create and photograph recipes, and there was Ivy, putting the finishing touches on an eighteen-layer chocolate cake. She called it a little layer cake (see pages 246 to 251), and a small crowd of recipe developers and food stylists had gathered to watch because they'd never heard of such a thing. Sounding like a seasoned cook far beyond her years, Ivy talked about the dessert's origins in parts of Georgia and Alabama and how her great-grandmother had often made it for special occasions. She and her mother had both grown up requesting it for their birthdays, and now she was hoping to make a version for *Southern Living* readers.

At the time, we were experimenting with different kinds of food videos online, so our longtime director, Mike Grady, asked if she'd like to re-create the cake in the studio the following week. All the recipes we were shooting back then were what we called "hands and pans"—very short and straight to the point—but Mike had a hunch about this one. He asked Ivy to tell the story behind the recipe and why it was important to her family. Like everyone else who watched it, I was charmed by her sense of humor, her enthusiasm, and her understanding of Southern culture. Ivy talked about the cake's history as she worked, carefully alternating each layer with a thin coating of chocolate frosting. Just as she'd done before, the finished product was a thing of beauty, but what stopped me in my tracks was the way she brought it to life on camera. Ivy wasn't just a talented cook or a budding video personality—she was a born storyteller.

The video went viral, of course, and Ivy has since become a fixture at *Southern Living*. She writes a popular column in the magazine, does food and drink demonstrations at events, appears on national television shows, and makes social media videos every week, sharing her cooking and entertaining tips. Her family has pitched in, too, whether it's her husband, Luis; her father, Wayne (who goes by Farmer WayneO); her mama, Sabrina; or her grandmother Judy (who's called Nana). Her house has become a video set as she's invited millions of *Southern Living* followers into her kitchen, and her recipes have helped a whole new generation of cooks with everything from weeknight dinners to holiday celebrations and Kentucky Derby parties.

I'm not sure what her secret is, but Ivy is an old soul who somehow, in her early thirties, speaks with the wisdom and authority of a Southern grandmother. She cooks with a confidence that can only come from countless hours in the kitchen, but she also understands why some recipes stir our emotions as well as our appetites. She loves the spirit of a Georgia Bulldog tailgate and the memories it conjures. She embraces quirky traditions like burying a bottle of bourbon to keep the rain away from a wedding, and she knows that the best recipes—like her Aunt Brenda's Sour Cream Banana Pudding (page 140)—are meant to be shared.

That's what this whole book is about. Like all the great Southern cooks and entertainers, Ivy realized a long time ago that her family stories and her recipes are inseparable. I hope you enjoy getting to know them both as much as I have.

—Sid Evans, Editor in Chief, *Southern Living*

introduction

If you ever need to find me, look in the kitchen first. I'm not hiding, I'm probably just hungry. The kitchen is where I go to unwind, get inspired, and feed the people I love. Whether I'm cooking in front of the camera, tasting a dish in the *Southern Living* Test Kitchen, or sharing a baking tip with fans, my job keeps me mostly in the kitchen—and I wouldn't have it any other way.

I was born and raised in rural South Georgia, and the house where I grew up was always a party. Our front door might as well have been a revolving one. Mama practically lived in the kitchen, making delicious dishes to feed the friends and family who were always stopping by. A pro with leftovers, she could repurpose a little of this and a little of that into something to satisfy hungry kids after school or a tray of nibbles for happy hour guests. Access to fancy ingredients wasn't guaranteed in our small town, so scrappiness was the name of her game. (And it still is for me today. I got that from her.)

Though Mama loved to host, Daddy was always the instigator of gatherings, big or small. He knew if he suggested a gathering at the house, he had to be ready to help make it happen—or at least stay out of Mama's way while she did. Where Mama is the ultimate host, Daddy is the ultimate *entertainer*. Sure, he occasionally helped with party menus by making his famous barbecue, but his self-appointed job at any Odom get-together was making sure everyone had a good time.

Like my parents, the way I cook and entertain is fun and approachable. It's also improvisational and creative, qualities I inherited from my mama. I love to share shortcuts to time-consuming classics, and though my hosting style is casual, I don't ever skimp on the wow factor.

While I graduated first in my class from culinary school at L'Academie de Cuisine in Gaithersburg, Maryland, and worked on the line in a fine-dining restaurant, my defining food moments have been in home kitchens all over the world. Traveling has played a huge role in how I eat, cook, and entertain. Though my parents' influence is strong, my style of hosting is entirely me. At *Southern Living*, my goal is to empower people to cook and entertain in their homes with confidence and minimal fuss. For anyone juggling work and social obligations, that kind of approach is critical. My husband, Luis, and I know a thing or two about busy social calendars. Like my dad when I was growing up, Luis is the instigator of most parties at our house. Together, we've figured out how to make hosting fun—and *mostly* stress-free. Taking notes from my mama, the best advice

I learned is to put everyone in the house to work come mealtime.

In these chapters, I've gathered more than one hundred of my favorite spins on classic Southern dishes, and I've organized them into occasion-focused chapters to reflect the many reasons Southerners gather, whether it be a casual weeknight supper with family or a lawn party for friends. While a few suggested menus appear throughout, all of the recipes are meant to be mixed, matched, and served for any occasion.

Throughout the book, you'll find "Ivy's Take!" and "Behind the Scenes"—nods to my work life in front of and behind the camera. These sidebars will feature advice and inspiration I've gleaned over the years in various kitchens—my childhood home, my culinary school, my video studio, and my own home kitchen. I'll share personal anecdotes, signature cooking secrets, fun ideas for setting the scene, and tried-and-true tips for hosting gatherings large and small. The "If This Isn't Southern . . ." sidebars are where I let you in on my go-to Southern staples I think are worth seeking out for your pantry too.

Every Southern kitchen and cook are different, and the way I make something might not be the same way you do. Though the recipes in this book have nostalgic familiarity, I've reinterpreted and refined them to provide a fun, new take or unexpected twist that I hope you will love as much as I do. They're simply suggestions and guides, so please use them in that way instead of following each and every one to a tee. My Southern kitchen isn't just mine—it's yours too. So come on in and make yourself at home.

4747 XJ
COLQUITT

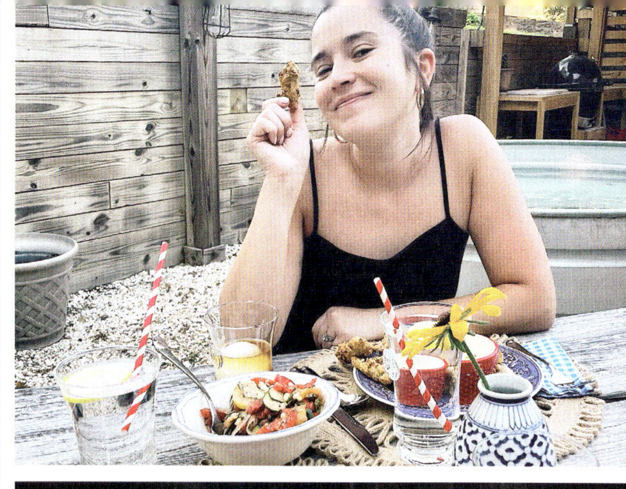

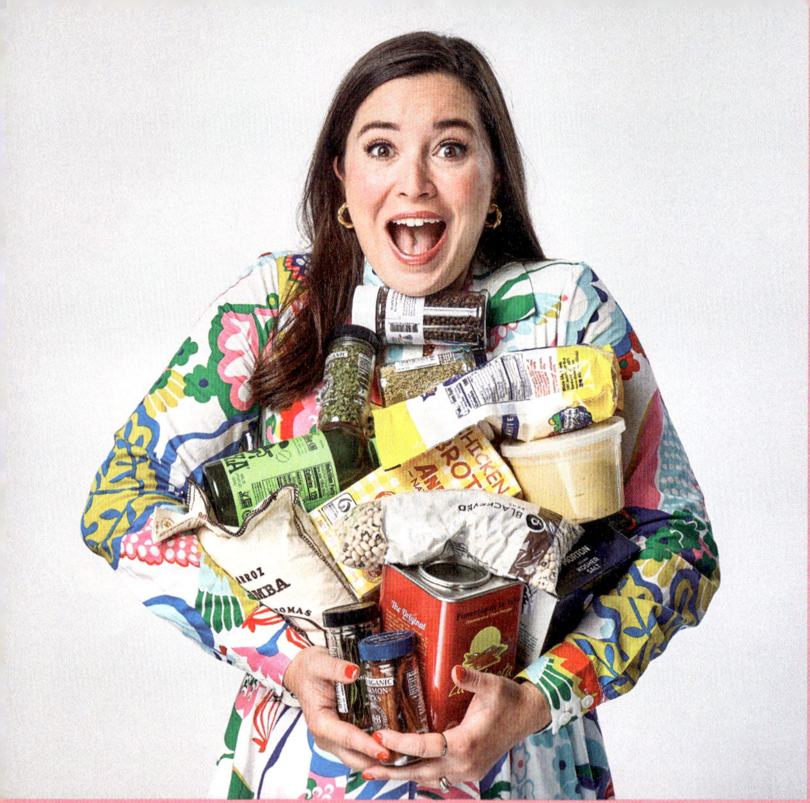
BLACKEYED

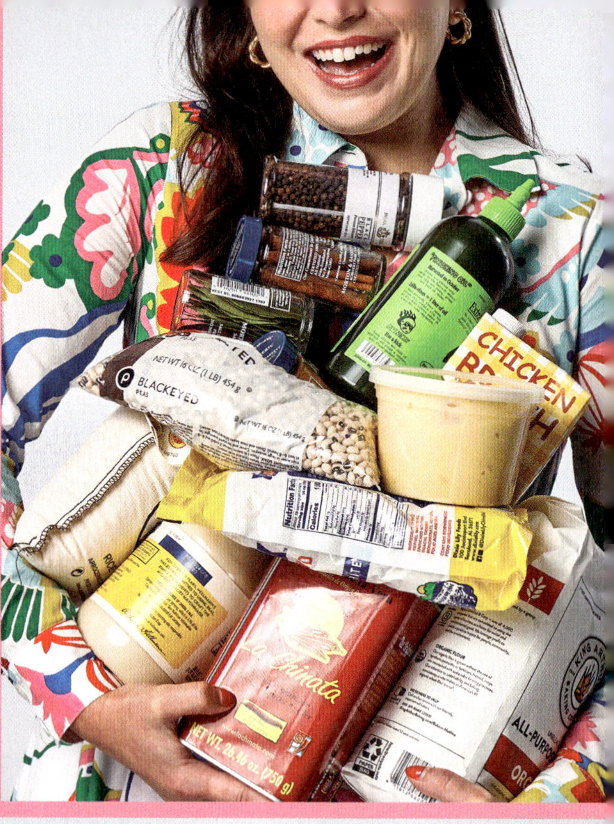
BLACKEYED
La Chinata

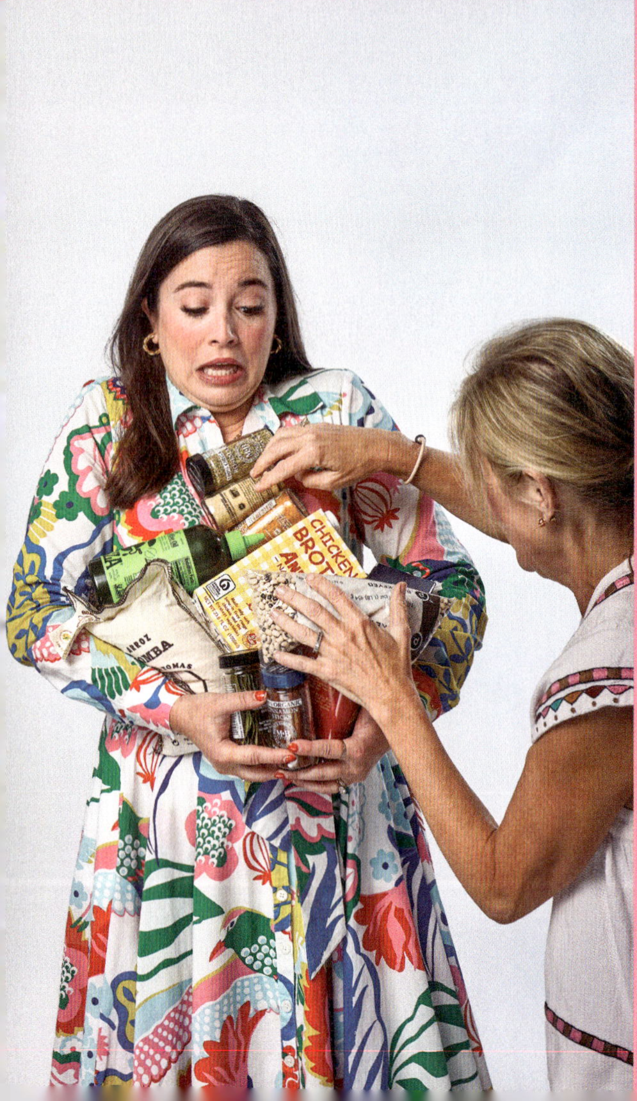

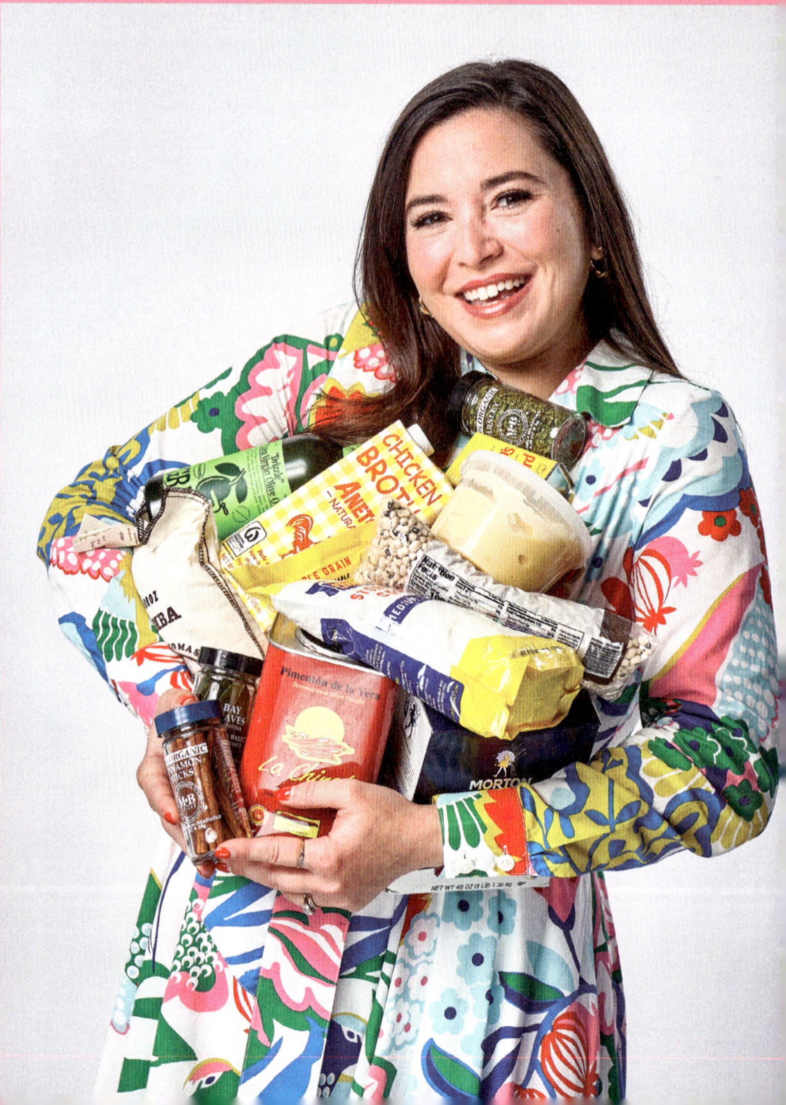
La Chinata
MORTON

chapter 1

my southern kitchen essentials

hen I set out to write this cookbook, I spent hours looking at my cookbook library. I love how some books incorporate family photos, others include essays about recipes that have personal meaning, and others offer helpful tips about how to perfect specific techniques or how to troubleshoot a recipe. All these features are implemented in my own way throughout the book, and each chapter follows a similar pattern with fun stories, silly photos, and culinary school–backed advice. That is, with the exception of this one. “My Southern Kitchen Essentials” is the real workhorse chapter of this book.

The recipes included in here are my staples: from the signature “house” blend of spices that I put on nearly everything, and the sauces and dressings I keep stocked in my fridge (with suggested uses for them in the recipes you will find later in the book) to homemade versions of some store-bought classics—plus one very essential recipe that my freezer would never be caught without. Listed at right are the things you’ll always find in my fridge and pantry. Keep these essentials on hand, mix yourself up a batch of House Seasoning (page 20), and I guarantee the dishes that come from your kitchen will taste a lot like those from mine.

ivy’s fridge and pantry staples

- chicken stock
- olive oil
- sweet Vidalia onions
- Yukon Gold potatoes
- fresh garlic head (not the minced in oil stuff!)
- local honey (or from my dad’s bees)
- Duke’s mayonnaise
- jarred pimientos
- Diamond Crystal kosher salt
- Wickles pickles
- panko breadcrumbs
- a variety of cornmeal: plain, self-rising, and finely ground
- Parmesan cheese
- heavy cream
- Dijon mustard
- bacon
- bacon grease
- lemons
- Worcestershire sauce
- butter (salted or unsalted as preferred)
- green onions
- a box of Ghirardelli brownie mix, just in case

house seasoning

MAKES ABOUT ½ CUP (48 G)
ACTIVE: 5 MINUTES
TOTAL: 5 MINUTES

3 tablespoons kosher salt

2 tablespoons smoked paprika

2 tablespoons garlic powder

1 tablespoon dried Italian seasoning

1 teaspoon freshly ground black pepper

Every kitchen has a house seasoning, even if the cook doesn't realize it. It's the go-to blend of herbs and spices you put on meats and veggies without even thinking about it. The amounts of each may vary if you don't premix your particular house blend. Even so, you habitually reach for these same seasonings when you cook. My special mix includes smoked paprika, garlic powder, Italian seasoning, salt, and pepper. When I'm making my Sunday Roasted Chicken (page 224), this seasoning is what I liberally sprinkle on the bird before it goes into the oven. When I need a quick side dish, this is the mix I'll toss almost any vegetable with before roasting. I keep a large container of house seasoning pre-mixed in my spice cabinet so I never have to think when cooking my weekly meals. The carefully concocted blend of savory flavors makes anything I cook quintessentially mine. If you find yourself constantly reaching for certain spice combinations, use this as encouragement to go ahead and mix up a bunch of them so that next time you have to get dinner on the table quickly, seasoning is one less thing you've got to do.

In a small bowl, stir together all ingredients until well-combined. Store in an airtight container up to 2 months.

---

ivy's take! I fell in love with smoked paprika when I lived in Spain. It has so much more flavor than regular paprika, and I have pretty much replaced regular paprika with it in all of my recipes. Here are a few jars to seek out:

- Spicewalla
- Chiquilín
- La Dalia
- Burlap & Barrel

I reach for House seasoning in these recipes:

- Cold Skillet Crispy Chicken Thighs (page 70)
- Weeknight Fried Chicken (page 73)
- Roasted Smashed Potatoes (page 94)
- Sunday Roasted Chicken (page 224)

browned butter

MAKES A SCANT 1 CUP (205 G)
ACTIVE: 10 MINUTES
TOTAL: 12 MINUTES

1 cup (225 g) salted butter

I started every morning at my (very French) culinary school by making clarified butter. It was the first thing I learned how to do, because it was the foundation for almost every recipe. Clarified butter is fairly simple to make. You melt butter in a saucepan over medium to medium-low heat, skimming off the milk solids as they float to the top. When all (or almost all, nobody is perfect) the milk solids have been skimmed, you're left with clarified butter—a flavorful fat that can withstand higher cooking temps than regular butter. After a few days in the classroom, I quickly learned that clarified butter can turn into beurre noisette (browned butter) in an instant if you're not careful. If the milk solids start to brown before they can be skimmed off, they turn nutty, making the butter take on a deep, aromatic flavor. Though my cooking instructor would gawk at my "ruined" pot of clarified butter and make me do it over again, he taught us that the best French chefs turn mistakes into something delicious. Browned butter can be used to deepen the flavor of many dishes, like my Freezer Chocolate Chip Cookies (page 37) or Browned Butter Mashed Potatoes (page 96). And while it might have originally been made by mistake, it certainly doesn't taste like one.

In a small saucepan, cook butter over medium heat until melted, about 5 minutes. Continue cooking over medium heat (butter will begin to foam; stir and reduce the heat to medium-low as needed so that it doesn't overflow) until butter starts to smell nutty and turn brown, 5 to 6 more minutes. Remove from heat and use immediately, or let cool completely and store in an airtight container in the refrigerator for up to 2 weeks.

roasted garlic butter

MAKES ABOUT ½ CUP (96 G)
ACTIVE: 10 MINUTES
TOTAL: 1 HOUR, 10 MINUTES

1 large head garlic

1 teaspoon extra-virgin olive oil

½ cup (115 g) salted butter, at room temperature

¼ teaspoon flaky salt

To me, one of the most annoying things in the world is sticky garlic husks (the papery outer layer of the garlic bulb). I wish I had a secret to avoiding it for this recipe, but I don't. If anyone knows one, please let me know. Until then, I'll be making my roasted garlic butter with sticky fingers. It's worth it.

1 Preheat oven to 350°F (175°C). Cut about ½ inch (12 mm) off the tip of the garlic head with a serrated knife to expose all garlic cloves, but leave the head fully intact. Drizzle cut side of garlic with olive oil and place garlic head, cut side up, into an 8 by 8-inch (20 by 20-cm) piece of aluminum foil. Bring edges of foil together and crimp to seal.

2 Roast garlic in preheated oven 45 to 50 minutes, until soft, creamy, and lightly golden brown. Remove from oven with tongs and keep garlic in foil until cool enough to handle, about 15 minutes.

3 Unwrap garlic from foil. Use tongs to squeeze roasted garlic cloves into a medium bowl (some of the sticky garlic skin might stubbornly get into the bowl, just be sure to pick it out). Add butter to the bowl and mash with a rubber spatula or fork until well-combined. Transfer to a serving dish and top with flaky salt.

serving tip: Serve with toasted bread or pizza crust for dipping, use it to make garlic bread, or spoon over a cooked steak just before serving.

shortcut garlic aioli

MAKES ABOUT ½ CUP (112 G)
ACTIVE: 5 MINUTES
TOTAL: 5 MINUTES

½ cup (120 ml) mayonnaise, such as Duke's

½ teaspoon grated garlic (from 1 medium clove)

½ teaspoon fresh lemon juice (from 1 lemon)

When Luis proposed to me, he sent me on a scavenger hunt around Birmingham to all our frequent date spots. The final clue led me to a beautiful place where our two office campuses met. At the time, he was working for Samford University, which neighbors the *Southern Living* headquarters in Homewood, Alabama. His proposal was sweet and so special. There were zinnias from my parents' garden, champagne sparkling in my great-grandmother's coupes, and the ring box my Papa used to propose to my Nana. I wouldn't change a thing about that day. But I most definitely would have said yes to Luis even if he'd proposed with a basket of fries and garlic aioli instead of a diamond ring. Because a good garlic dipping sauce is one of the simplest joys in life. Luis and I love it so much we served it with fries as our late-night snack during our wedding reception. This shortcut version takes less than 5 minutes, and come to think of it, maybe I should've named it "Marry Me Garlic Aioli," because it's just that good.

In a small bowl, stir all ingredients together. Serve immediately, or store in an airtight container in the refrigerator until ready to use, up to 5 days.

serving tip: Serve with Roasted Smashed Potatoes (page 94), on a burger, with pizza crust, with crudités, or with anything else that needs a yummy dipping sauce.

goes-on-everything balsamic syrup

MAKES ABOUT ¼ CUP (60 ML)
ACTIVE: 7 MINUTES
TOTAL: 7 MINUTES

½ cup (120 ml) balsamic vinegar

3 tablespoons packed light brown sugar

⅛ teaspoon kosher salt

One of my husband's most-requested dinners is some sort of chicken, a roasted vegetable, and a salad. Though he eats pretty much anything I cook for him, his top requests always err on the simpler–ahem, boring–side. After a few too many average meals, I asked if he'd be OK if I changed it up a little. I made a quick batch of this easy balsamic syrup and drizzled it over our chicken and veggies, and now he requests it every time. It adds just enough sweet and tart flavors to balance out a dish, and it is my go-to condiment for making just about anything a little less boring.

In a medium skillet, cook vinegar and sugar over medium-high heat, whisking occasionally, until thick and syrupy and reduced by half, 5 to 7 minutes. Stir in salt. Serve immediately.

---

serving tip: Goes-on-everything balsamic syrup literally could go on everything, but some of my favorites include: Cold Skillet Crispy Chicken Thighs (page 70); Sunday Roasted Chicken (page 224); Fried Summer Vegetables (page 162); Tomato, Cucumber, and Onion Salad (page 81); or as a topping or drizzle for pizza, sliced peaches, burrata, or vanilla ice cream (trust me!).

if this isn't southern . . . I'm in the stage of life where I'm keeping the meal train circuit hot. In the South, we can run a meal train like it's our second job. I've included a whole chapter on meals for times like these starting on page 107, because we all need ideas beyond creamy chicken noodle casserole. I love to make baked chicken for meal trains, and every time the recipients always ask for the recipe because, "I've never had baked chicken this good!" The secret is this balsamic syrup. When the chicken comes out of the oven, spoon a little on top, and you'll start getting asked about your secret, too.

hot honey mustard

MAKES ABOUT ½ CUP (120 ML)
ACTIVE: 15 MINUTES
TOTAL: 15 MINUTES

2 tablespoons English mustard powder, such as Colman's

1 tablespoon cold water

¼ cup (60 ml) honey

2 tablespoons mayonnaise

1 teaspoon canola oil

¼ teaspoon crushed red pepper

⅛ teaspoon kosher salt

Like many kids, I grew up on a diet of chicken tenders and french fries. It wasn't my mama's fault. She tried relentlessly to get me to eat anything other than fried chicken, saying if I didn't start eating different foods I'd grow feathers out of my ears. I've since grown out of my chicken-fingers-only diet, but based on the number of chicken recipes I've included in this book (it's twelve, but who's counting?), the jury is still out on whether or not I'll start sprouting feathers. In all my years of chicken eating, I've become a dipping sauce connoisseur. My go-to is honey mustard. This hot version has a strong kick that I wouldn't have appreciated during my early years, but now it's a welcome upgrade for those times when nothing but a basket of chicken tenders will do.

In a medium bowl, whisk together mustard powder and water until smooth. Let stand 10 minutes. Whisk in remaining ingredients until smooth. Serve immediately, or store in an airtight container in the refrigerator for up to 5 days. (As is, this honey mustard has a kick that will clear out your sinuses. If you find it too strong, just cut both the amount of mustard and the amount of water in half.)

---

note: Did you know dry mustard powder needs water to activate? If you were to mix everything together without giving the mustard the 10-minute activation time, it would taste like nothing. Trust me, I've tried it.

serving tip: Hot honey mustard is great with Weeknight Fried Chicken (page 73), Roasted Smashed Potatoes (page 94), or as a condiment for your favorite takeout tender basket.

our favorite salad dressing

MAKES ABOUT ⅔ CUP (165 ML)
ACTIVE: 5 MINUTES
TOTAL: 5 MINUTES

2 tablespoons balsamic vinegar

1 tablespoon honey

1 tablespoon Dijon mustard

6 tablespoons (90 ml) extra-virgin olive oil

½ teaspoon kosher salt

¼ teaspoon freshly ground black pepper

Please stop buying store-bought salad dressing. Unless it's ranch, you should make salad dressing at home. (Though I could argue homemade ranch is also better.) It's way more delicious than the bottled stuff and takes all of 5 minutes to make. Like many others in the book, this recipe is simply a starting point for you to take in any direction you want. Switch up the vinegar for citrus juice, leave out the honey or substitute it with maple syrup, throw in some herbs or poppy seeds, or stir in a tablespoon of mayo to make it creamy. Who knows, maybe you'll come up with your own favorite salad dressing in the process.

In a medium bowl, whisk together balsamic vinegar, honey, and mustard. Slowly drizzle in olive oil, whisking constantly, until dressing is emulsified. Season with salt and pepper. Store in an airtight container in the refrigerator for up to 1 week.

easy freezer tomato sauce

MAKES 5 CUPS (1.2 L)
ACTIVE: 1 HOUR
TOTAL: 1 HOUR, 30 MINUTES

5 pounds (2.3 kg) ripe tomatoes (about 10 medium tomatoes), quartered

2 teaspoons kosher salt

As a Southerner from a farming community, I feel some sort of duty to be an expert in canning. Maybe it's because I grew up in a house with an overflowing garden and graduated with a degree in home economics from the University of Georgia, home of the National Center for Home Food Preservation to boot. Or maybe it's because the county where I'm from has a canning plant open to the public five days a week during peak harvest season. But, if I'm being honest, I'm no canning expert. In fact, I would go so far as to say I really don't like it. I mean, have y'all ever canned anything before?

There's the sterilization, the slippery tongs that precariously maneuver breakable glass jars or containers over boiling hot water, and the overarching fear of food safety that looms over the whole to-do. It's all a bit too much for me. This is why when putting up time comes for my little garden, I will freeze, juice, or quick-pickle a vegetable ten times before I'll can it. My recipe for freezer tomato sauce is so much easier than the traditional method. Not only does it avoid the daunting jar boiling, it also uses the whole tomato, skins and all, for a quick, fuss-free sauce that can be used in many recipes. It's my answer for preserving the season without all the rigmarole, because putting up shouldn't be something to put up with.

1 Working in 3 batches, place quartered tomatoes in a food processor bowl and pulse until finely chopped, about 15 pulses.

2 Transfer finely chopped tomatoes to a 4-quart (3.8-L) Dutch oven and cook over medium-high heat, stirring occasionally, until reduced by half, about 30 minutes.

3 Remove Dutch oven from heat. Using an immersion blender, blend tomatoes until smooth, about 1 minute. (You can also use a regular blender, working in batches, but be careful to leave room for steam in the lid if you go this route).

4 Return Dutch oven to heat, reduce heat to medium, and cook, stirring occasionally, until sauce is reduced to 5 cups (1.2 L) and slightly thickened, about 10 minutes. Remove from heat and stir in salt. Ladle into freezer-safe, airtight containers, and let cool completely before closing and storing. Store sauce in freezer up to 1 year. Thaw completely before using.

homemade cream of chicken soup

MAKES 6½ CUPS (1.5 L)
ACTIVE: 15 MINUTES
TOTAL: 45 MINUTES

½ cup (115 g) unsalted butter

1¼ cups (155 g) all-purpose flour

3¾ cups (900 ml) low-sodium chicken broth

2 cups (489 ml) whole milk

2 teaspoons premium roasted chicken paste, such as Better Than Bouillon

1 teaspoon kosher salt

1 teaspoon onion powder

1 teaspoon garlic powder

Turns out when you're in the middle of making Green Chile Chicken Enchiladas (page 139) and realize your pantry is slap out of canned cream of chicken soup, you can quickly make your own. This recipe was born out of necessity, but it has stuck around because of its usefulness. As soon as I use up my last frozen container of cream of chicken soup, I add it to my prep list for my next Sunday meal prep day. It's easy to make and can be used in place of the can in any recipe, so it's one less thing you have to add to your grocery list.

1. In a medium saucepan, melt butter over medium heat. Whisk in flour (mixture will become a thick, dry, clumpy dough ball) and continue cooking, stirring constantly, until raw flour smell has dissipated, about 1 minute.

2. Gradually whisk in chicken broth, a little at a time, whisking in each addition fully before adding the next. Whisk in milk and bouillon paste until completely smooth. Continue cooking over medium until mixture thickens to a pudding-like consistency, 3 to 4 minutes. Be careful not to let the mixture come to a rolling boil.

3. Remove from heat, then stir in salt, onion powder, and garlic powder. Divide soup evenly among 6 freezer-safe containers. (Each container should get about 1 cup / 240 ml). Let soup cool in containers to room temperature before closing and storing in the freezer for up to 3 months.

4. Thawing instructions: Take container out of the freezer and place in the refrigerator overnight to thaw completely. (When using thawed soup, mixture may separate when heated. Add in about ¼ cup / 60 ml whole or evaporated milk to bring it back together, if desired.) Note: Make sure to use evaporated milk, not sweetened condensed milk, if you choose that option.

Cream of
Cream of Chicken
Soup

lemon curd

MAKES ABOUT 3 CUPS (720 ML)
ACTIVE: 30 MINUTES
TOTAL: 4 HOURS, 30 MINUTES

12 egg yolks

2¼ cups (450 g) granulated sugar

2 tablespoons cornstarch, optional (see note)

1 tablespoon grated lemon zest plus ¾ cup (180 ml) fresh juice (from 5 large lemons)

¼ teaspoon kosher salt

¾ cup (170 g) cold unsalted butter, cut into ½-inch (12 mm) pieces

While I could eat lemon curd by the spoonful, this recipe was originally created to be the filling for my Lemon-Cheese Layer Cake (page 249). It's also great as a topper for Pavlovas (page 259), or spooned over store-bought cheesecake for an impressive, easy dessert.

1. In a medium heavy saucepan, whisk together egg yolks, granulated sugar, cornstarch (if using), lemon zest and juice, and salt until combined. Cook over medium heat, stirring constantly with a wooden spoon, until mixture is thick and coats the back of the spoon, 8 to 10 minutes. Remove from heat. Add cold butter; stir until melted and smooth.

2. Pour mixture through a fine mesh strainer into a medium bowl; discard any lumps. Place bowl with strained lemon curd filling into a large bowl filled with ice water. Let stand, stirring often, until mixture is cool, about 20 minutes. Remove medium bowl from ice water bowl and place a piece of plastic wrap directly on top of filling (to prevent a film from forming). Cover and chill until filling is firm, at least 4 hours or up to 3 days.

ivy's take! To make this into a cake filling, use the cornstarch listed in the ingredient list. The cornstarch will thicken the curd enough to hold up in a cake. If you'd prefer a more spoonable curd to use as a topping, simply omit the cornstarch and proceed with the recipe as directed.

herb simple syrup

MAKES ABOUT 1 CUP (240 ML)
ACTIVE: 10 MINUTES
TOTAL: 40 MINUTES

½ cup (100 g) granulated sugar

½ cup (120 ml) water

½ cup (25 g) packed fresh basil or mint leaves, or ½ cup (25 g) fresh thyme or rosemary sprigs

Luis and I keep flavored simple syrup in our fridge pretty much at all times. We love to use it in our Brown Water Friday happy hour cocktails. While we're partial to the basil version (see our Bourbon-Basil Smash on page 44), it's fun to switch up the herbs with the seasons. You'd be surprised how delicious a thyme simple syrup is for an old-fashioned! Leftover simple syrup can be drizzled over fresh fruit or brushed on cakes to keep them moist, but you can easily cut the recipe in half to prevent leftovers.

In a small saucepan, combine all ingredients and cook over medium heat, stirring occasionally, just until sugar dissolves, about 5 minutes. Remove from heat and let cool completely to room temperature, about 30 minutes. Strain through a fine mesh strainer, discarding the herbs, and store in an airtight container in the refrigerator for up to 1 week.

freezer chocolate chip cookies (yes, these are essential!)

MAKES 3 DOZEN
ACTIVE: 30 MINUTES
TOTAL: 1 DAY, 45 MINUTES, INCLUDING 1 DAY CHILLING

1 cup (205 g) browned butter, softened (page 23)

1⅓ cups (295 g) packed dark brown sugar

⅓ cup (65 g) granulated sugar

2 large eggs, at room temperature

2 teaspoons vanilla extract

2½ cups (315 g) all-purpose flour

½ cup (45 g) uncooked quick-cooking oats

1 teaspoon baking powder

½ teaspoon baking soda

1½ cups (12 ounces / 340 g) bittersweet or semisweet chocolate chunks

½ cup (4 ounces / 113 g) bittersweet or semisweet chocolate chips

Flaky sea salt, such as Maldon

Sometimes, you just need a cookie—or a dessert for a last-minute gathering. Whatever the emergency may be, a batch of frozen chocolate chip cookie dough is the answer. I keep these in my freezer at all times, which is why I've included them in my Essentials chapter. Sometimes I bake them, and sometimes I don't. What you choose to do is your business.

1 Using a heavy-duty electric stand mixer, beat butter, brown sugar, and granulated sugar on medium-high speed until light and fluffy, about 3 minutes. Add eggs, one at a time; beat until well-combined after each addition. Beat until fluffy, about 1 minute. Beat in vanilla. In a small bowl, stir together flour, oats, baking powder, and baking soda. Gradually add to butter mixture, beating until well-blended. Stir in chocolate.

2 Using a 3-tablespoon scoop, drop spoonfuls of dough onto a parchment paper–lined baking sheet (it's okay if the cookies touch). Freeze scooped cookies until frozen all the way through, 1 to 2 hours. Transfer frozen cookies to an airtight container and store in the freezer for up to 3 months.

3 When ready to bake, take out desired amount of cookies from the freezer (even if you just want one—I'm not judging, I've done this plenty of times!). Place cookies 2 inches (5 cm) apart on a parchment paper–lined baking sheet, then preheat the oven to 375°F (190°C). Bake cookies in preheated oven until edges are golden and bottoms are set, but cookies are still soft to the touch, 11 to 13 minutes.

4 Remove cookies from oven and sprinkle with a generous pinch of flaky salt; cool on baking sheets on wire racks for 5 minutes. Serve warm, or transfer cookies to wire racks to cool completely, about 20 minutes.

behind the scenes These cookies have gone through a few iterations in order to achieve chocolate chip cookie perfection. I swapped the original light brown sugar for dark. This helped a lot, but when I ate the raw cookie dough (for legal reasons I cannot endorse this), I felt like they needed something else to take them over the top. Enter browned butter. By taking the few extra minutes to brown the butter, you get a cookie-dough ball packed with rich, nutty flavor that's delicious right out of the freezer (but again, I cannot recommend, for legal purposes) and perfect when baked, too!

chapter 2

cheers, y’all!

s a woman who's really into bourbon, hunting down the hard-to-find-in-Alabama bottles on road trips with my husband is so much fun. I love sipping it neat or on the rocks, but I know it can be polarizing for many people. Maybe it's the thought that it's too heavy, too singular, or just for the boys. But I say, why should we leave all the fun to them? When guests came up to me during our wedding reception saying they couldn't believe how much they liked our signature bourbon-based cocktail (page 44), I knew immediately I had to come up with more bourbon drinks that would turn non-bourbon drinkers on to our beloved Brown Water.

Luis and I love to celebrate Brown Water Fridays, which is just a term used for drinking a bourbon cocktail at the end of the work week. A lot of the cocktails in this chapter are bourbon-based because we are constantly trying to find new ways to enjoy our beloved spirit. You might be surprised to find they're all surprisingly light, refreshing, and approachable—adjectives not normally used to describe whiskey drinks.

There are plenty of drinks in this chapter that don't use bourbon or any booze at all. Whether you need a crowd-pleasing punch for a shower (page 53), or a frozen slush for a summer party (page 61), you'll find a drink for everyone and every occasion here. Given my Southern roots, I couldn't let a drink chapter go by without telling you how to make a proper pitcher of the "table wine of the South." Though some disagree—the secret to the best sweet tea is baking soda. You can read more about that on page 57. These drinks can also be found on a few of my featured party menus throughout the book. Some of them are occasion-focused, like the Masters Azalea Cocktail on page 63, and others are made for good old-fashioned porch sipping. I hope you enjoy them as much as I do. Cheers, y'all!

Weller
THE ORIGINAL
WHEATED BOURBON
SPECIAL RESERV

Basil Smash
lemon
basil
agave
gin or Bourbon
Maker's Mark
Tanqueray

When most people think about their wedding day, they remember it fondly. Ours is no exception. Though it wasn't perfect, because nothing ever is, it was pretty darn close. The ceremony was in the church I grew up in, and the reception was under a sailcloth tent pitched in my parents' yard. There was a nine-piece brass band, a black-and-white checkered dance floor, and hundreds of flowers set beautifully in bud vases throughout the entire space. The menu was a mix of Southern and Spanish cuisines. There was fried chicken, seafood paella, a whole hog, deviled eggs, pimiento cheese and Íberico ham, among a slew of other tapas and sides. Everything about it was fun and memorable, and thanks to a quirky Southern wedding superstition, the weather could not have been more perfect.

Legend has it that if you bury a bottle of bourbon upside down at the site of your wedding a month before you say your vows, the weather on your wedding day will be beautiful. In keeping with this Southern tradition, Luis and I dug a hole in my parents' yard (FYI: It's frowned upon to bury bourbon in the yard of a church by the way), placed a bottle of Weller Special Reserve in a bag upside down in the hole, and covered it right back up.

After the wedding, while Luis and I were busy digging up the bottle (in my white dress to boot), the rest of our guests were enjoying our signature wedding cocktail. Guests had the choice of bourbon or gin as a base spirit, but it's safe to say the bourbon was the real crowd-pleaser.

Affectionately named the Basil Smash after our dog, Basil, the cocktail was a perfectly crafted concoction of bourbon (or gin), basil, lemon, and agave syrup that our guests are still raving about years later. Luis and I were too busy talking to people to really enjoy it during our reception, which is why we love to mix it at home and reminisce about that best day. We keep our wedding cocktail sign, painted by the lovely Merryn Williams, in our kitchen as a daily reminder to thank God for bourbon and no rain!

bourbon-basil smash

SERVES 2
ACTIVE: 10 MINUTES
TOTAL: 45 MINUTES

½ cup (100 g) granulated sugar

½ cup (120 ml) water

½ cup (25 g) packed fresh basil leaves, plus 8 additional leaves, divided

½ cup (109 g) ice, plus more for serving

½ cup (4 ounces / 120 ml) bourbon

¼ cup (60 ml) fresh lemon juice (from 2 lemons)

Basil sprigs, for garnish

Lemon slices, for garnish

Luis and I have quite the bourbon collection. Our harder-to-find bourbons are reserved for sipping neat or on the rocks, but these bottles are our go-tos for sipping and mixing drinks for our Brown Water Fridays: Woodford Reserve, Blade and Bow, Buffalo Trace, and Elijah Craig Small Batch.

1. In a small saucepan, bring sugar, water, and ½ cup (25 g) of the basil to a boil over medium heat. Boil until sugar dissolves, about 2 minutes. Remove from heat and let cool completely, about 30 minutes. Pour basil simple syrup through a fine mesh strainer into a small heatproof container, discarding leaves.

2. Muddle remaining 8 basil leaves in bottom of a cocktail shaker using a muddler or handle of a wooden spoon. Add ½ cup (109 g) ice to cocktail shaker with bourbon, lemon juice, and 3 tablespoons basil simple syrup. (Reserve remaining syrup for another use.) Add lid to shaker, then shake vigorously until chilled, about 30 seconds. Fill two lowball glasses with additional ice. Pour cocktail through fine mesh strainer evenly into glasses, and garnish each with a basil sprig and lemon slice.

if this isn't southern . . . One of my new cocktail ingredient obsessions is orgeat. It's a syrup typically made from almonds, sweetened and flavored with citrus and floral essences. While I love orgeat in any form, one of my absolute favorites is made by El Guapo, a New Orleans–based company that specializes in unique cocktail ingredients. Their Creole Orgeat is made from pecans grown in southern Georgia in place of the usual almonds, and it is perfect for adding to old-fashioneds, milk punch, and tiki drinks like this one.

frozen bourbon painkiller

SERVES 4
ACTIVE: 10 MINUTES
TOTAL: 2 HOURS, 10 MINUTES

2 cups (480 ml) pineapple juice

1 cup (8 ounces / 240 ml) bourbon

1 cup (240 ml) cream of coconut (from one 15-ounce / 425-g can)

½ cup (120 ml) fresh orange juice (from 2 navel oranges)

¼ cup (60 ml) orgeat syrup (my favorite is El Guapo Creole Orgeat)

2 tablespoons honey

¼ teaspoon ground cinnamon

4 cups (870 g) ice

Freshly grated nutmeg, fresh pineapple wedges, and pineapple leaves, for garnish

The Blue Sky Grill in my hometown of Moultrie, Georgia, was known for its "stress reliever" cocktail. It was a sweet, refreshing, a-little-too-easy-to-drink concoction that definitely got rid of anything that ailed you. It was my mama's usual order on a weekend night out, and it was on the top of my list of cocktails to try when I reached drinking age. It definitely lived up to the hype. Fast forward a few years and I learned that lots of bars serve drinks claiming to relieve stress or kill pain. My version of a painkiller cocktail is an ode to the Blue Sky's stress reliever and a riff on the classic painkiller. The bourbon and warm spices add a depth of flavor that will knock your socks off. It goes down easy and takes away all the pain, at least just for a moment.

1. In a blender, process pineapple juice, bourbon, cream of coconut, orange juice, orgeat syrup, honey, and cinnamon on low speed until smooth, about 10 seconds. Cover blender container tightly with plastic wrap and place in freezer until very cold, at least 2 hours.

2. Add ice to mixture in blender and process on high speed until thick and frothy, about 1 minute. Divide among 4 glasses; garnish each with grated nutmeg, a pineapple wedge, and pineapple leaves.

bourbon mule

SERVES 1
ACTIVE: 5 MINUTES
TOTAL: 5 MINUTES

1 cup (217 g) ice

¼ cup (2 ounces / 60 ml) bourbon

1 tablespoon fresh lime juice (from 1 lime)

½ cup (120 ml) nonalcoholic ginger beer (from one 12.7-ounce / 375-ml bottle)

Mint sprig, for garnish

While I do love a Moscow mule, I love it with bourbon even more. But trust me when I say, I don't recommend serving this with the copper straws that come with your mugs—unless you want to recreate the tongue-stuck-to-a-flagpole scene from the film *A Christmas Story*.

Fill a copper mule mug or silver julep cup with ice. Add bourbon and lime juice; stir. Top with ginger beer. Garnish with a mint sprig.

GOOD LUCK
GOOD LUCK
2020
USHJA
2022

derby party

serving suggestions

When I think of the Kentucky Derby, fashion comes to mind way before the horses. A fancy hat instantly suggests, "I'm going to Churchill Downs." There's no other statement piece quite like it. When I'm at home watching the race, I re-create the fanfare of the event as closely as I can by pulling out my silver julep cups, putting on a brightly colored dress and coordinating hat, and making an extravagant menu to match.

While no Derby menu is complete without mint juleps, this bourbon-lover also likes to set out ingredients for people to make their own Bourbon Mules (page 47), so I don't have to play bartender throughout the party. I'm convinced all proper Southern parties must have deviled eggs, no excuses! Find my recipe for the classic style on page 165, or serve them all gussied up with topping "fascinators." My Hot Brown Party Rolls (page 169) were made for celebrating the Run for the Roses, so break out the Hawaiian rolls and head off to the races!

PLAZA DE TOROS MONUMENTAL DE MADRID
Grandiosa Corrida de Toros
6 HERMOSOS TOROS, 6
JULIO APARICIO
JAIME OSTOS
ANDRES VAZQUEZ
derby day
mint juleps
deviled eggs
brownies

triple-b milk punch

SERVES 12
ACTIVE: 5 MINUTES
TOTAL: 35 MINUTES, INCLUDING CHILLING

3 cups (720 ml) cold whole milk

1½ cups (12 ounces / 360 ml) bourbon, chilled

1½ cups (12 ounces / 360 ml) brandy, chilled

1½ cups (360 ml) cold whole buttermilk

¾ cup (180 ml) honey

1½ teaspoons vanilla extract

4 cinnamon sticks

1 medium orange, thinly sliced

Freshly grated nutmeg

Ice, for serving

In many parts of the South, we don't really know what it's like to have a white Christmas. Where I'm from, just two counties north of the Georgia-Florida line, Christmases are in fact often pretty warm. If you've ever tried shopping for holiday outfits in the South, you'll know the dilemma of scouring boutiques for something that's seasonably appropriate yet not likely to cause unnecessary glistening. That's why I love a white Christmas party. It's the one chance between Labor Day and Easter that we get to whip out a good white dress and still be fashionable. Decking halls and donning apparel in an all-white scheme are classic and elegant ways to get everyone in the spirit. It might also help if you mix up a batch of this boozy Triple-B milk punch. The punch gets its name from three ingredients that make up the cocktail: bourbon, brandy, and buttermilk. One cool and creamy sip might not bring a white Christmas, but it may make your days merry and bright.

In a gallon pitcher, whisk together milk, bourbon, brandy, buttermilk, honey, and vanilla until combined. Chill at least 30 minutes or up to 1 week. Pour into a punch bowl. Add cinnamon sticks and orange slices, and garnish with nutmeg. Serve over ice.

mama jane's coffee punch

MAKES ABOUT 14 CUPS (3.3 L)
ACTIVE: 15 MINUTES
TOTAL: 25 MINUTES

3 pints (1.4 L) vanilla ice cream, such as Blue Bell Homemade Vanilla

6 tablespoons (43 g) instant coffee

½ cup (120 ml) hot water

1 cup (240 ml) chocolate syrup, such as Hershey's Special Dark, plus more for garnish

⅛ teaspoon kosher salt

6 cups (1.4 L) cold whole milk

This recipe comes from Jane Gibbs, affectionately known all over Moultrie, Georgia, as Mama Jane. If we had royalty in Moultrie, she'd definitely be the queen. A lot of my love for cooking and hosting came from women like her. A former home economics teacher and church hostess, she has a knack for showing people love through being hospitable. Whether it's serving the entire football team Packer Skor cake, fittingly made with Skor candy bars, before a game or greeting everyone as they walked through the fellowship hall doors for Wednesday night supper, Mama Jane knew the secret to hospitality was good food and a smile. Almost every wedding and baby shower I've ever been to in Moultrie has served Mama Jane's mocha ice cream punch. It's just not a shower without it. I'm so privileged to be able to share it with y'all so that a little bit of Mama Jane can live in your kitchen, too.

1 Remove ice cream from the freezer and let sit at room temperature 15 to 20 minutes to soften before making punch. Meanwhile, in a large bowl or 8-cup (2-L) measuring cup, whisk together instant coffee and hot water until dissolved. Whisk in chocolate syrup and salt until smooth, then whisk in milk.

2 Transfer softened ice cream to a large pitcher. Pour one-third of the coffee mixture into the pitcher and whisk until it reaches the consistency of a thick milkshake. Add in the remaining coffee mixture and whisk until smooth.

3 Drizzle chocolate syrup along the sides of a punch bowl. Pour punch into punch bowl, then drizzle more chocolate syrup on top of punch before serving.

spicy pineapple margaritas

SERVES 2
ACTIVE: 10 MINUTES
TOTAL: 10 MINUTES

½ large jalapeño, thinly sliced (or 1 small)

¼ cup (2 ounces / 60 ml) Plain Simple Syrup (recipe follows)

½ cup (109 g) ice, plus more for serving

6 tablespoons (3 ounces / 90 ml) blanco tequila

5 tablespoons (2½ ounces / 75 ml) pineapple juice

¼ cup (2 ounces / 60 ml) lime juice (from 2 limes—save lime halves for rimming the glasses)

1 tablespoon (½ ounce / 15 ml) orange liqueur, such as Cointreau or triple sec

1 pinch kosher salt

Tajín or salt, for rimming glasses

Limes, pineapple wedges, or jalapeño slices, for garnish (optional)

Luis and I frequent happy hour at a local Tex-Mex spot with two of our best friends, Cole and Betsy. Our orders are always the same: spicy pineapple margaritas for me and Luis, house margaritas for Cole and Betsy, queso and guacamole for the table. When five o'clock rolls around and it's been a long day for one of the four of us, we text the group and everyone assembles just in the nick of time to get a drink before happy hour ends at six. While the restaurant infuses their tequila with jalapeños overnight, my version speeds it up so that in the event we miss happy hour by a few minutes, we have an easy way to recreate it at home.

1. In a cocktail shaker, muddle together jalapeño and simple syrup until jalapeño is well mashed. Add ½ cup (109 g) ice to cocktail shaker, along with tequila, pineapple juice, lime juice, orange liqueur, and pinch of salt. Use your saved juiced lime halves or wedges to rub along the rim of two serving glasses. Sprinkle Tajín or salt onto a small plate, then dip the rim of each glass into the Tajín or salt to coat, twirling the glass for more coverage. Fill glasses with ice.
2. Close lid and shake until very chilled, about 30 seconds. When your hands are frozen, the margarita is cold enough!
3. Strain into serving glasses. Garnish, if desired. Cheers!

plain simple syrup

MAKES ½ CUP (120 ML)

½ cup (100 g) granulated sugar

½ cup (120 ml) water

In a small saucepan, bring sugar and water to a boil over medium-high heat. Cook, stirring often, 1 minute, or until sugar dissolves completely. Remove from heat and let cool completely. Store in an airtight container in the refrigerator up to 2 weeks.

pomegranate ranch water

SERVES 1
ACTIVE: 5 MINUTES
TOTAL: 5 MINUTES

¼ cup (60 ml) blanco tequila

6 tablespoons (90 ml) sparkling water, such as Topo Chico

2 tablespoons fresh lime juice

2 teaspoons bottled pomegranate juice

Lime wheel, for garnish

Ranch water is one of *Southern Living*'s most popular recipes, if you could even call it a recipe. It's a Texas favorite that just mixes tequila with Topo Chico and a squeeze of lime. It's very refreshing, but I love to add a little flavor boost with some seasonal fruit juice. One of my favorites is pomegranate, but it's equally good with peach, watermelon, or strawberry.

Fill a double old-fashioned or rocks glass with ice. Add blanco tequila, sparkling water, lime juice, and bottled pomegranate juice. Stir to combine. Garnish with a lime wheel.

lime-beer shandy

SERVES 6
ACTIVE: 5 MINUTES
TOTAL: 5 MINUTES

4 (12-ounce / 360-ml) cans chilled Mexican-style lager, such as Corona or Stone Buenaveza

4 cups (960 ml) cold limeade, such as Simply Limeade

Ice, for serving

Lime slices, for garnish

I'm not the biggest beer person. Hoppy IPAs and dark stouts are not my idea of refreshing, but I do enjoy the occasional lager or fruit-flavored ale. For parties, this beer shandy (shown on page 150) is an affordable, delicious way to serve beer to a crowd that will even please the non-beer drinkers on the guest list.

In a gallon-size pitcher, stir together beer and limeade. Serve over ice with lime slices.

basil
agave
gin or bourbon
the Southern Living COMMUNITY COOKBOOK

Sweet tea is known as the "table wine of the South." While the French may think wine is necessary for a good dinner, a proper Southern supper isn't complete without a pitcher of tea on the table. Like most Southern children, I grew up on sweet tea. If I wasn't careful, I'd drink so much I'd make myself sick. On an empty stomach, syrupy-sweet tea is not the best move. The sugar and the tannins really can do a number on you if you aren't careful. Tea, by nature, is bitter from tannins (natural compounds found in leaves, bark, and fruit). Tea-drinkers across the globe have learned ways to combat this natural bitterness by adding sugar, cream, or citrus to make their cup of caffeine more enjoyable. Southerners have been adding sugar to their iced tea for hundreds of years, but there is another ingredient that many know is the real secret to cut the bitterness: baking soda.

Our official *Southern Living* recipe for making proper Southern-style sweet tea calls for adding this controversial ingredient to the steeping tea bags in order to help cut the bitterness and make the tea less cloudy. One of my very first *Southern Living* videos showed followers this method, but based on their reaction, you would've thought I told them to put sugar in their cornbread (a cardinal sin in a real Southern kitchen!). A single pinch of baking soda in a pitcher of tea sent everyone into a tizzy. Some commenters ran to my defense saying their grandmother made tea this way, but most were appalled. "I have lived in the South my whole life, and I have NEVER had tea like this!," "My MeeMaw is rolling in her grave," and "Are we SURE she's Southern? This is just wrong!" Now that's just a few among the thousands of comments we received on the topic. It went so viral, people came up to me in public asking if I was the *Southern Living* Sweet Tea Girl, and more than four years later people are still commenting on our videos asking, "Where's the baking soda?"

Southern grandmothers have been adding baking soda to their tea pitchers for generations, but as soon as I told their secret in our viral video, fans have wanted to revoke my Southern card more times than I can count for various kitchen crimes. But if I'm not Southern, I don't know who is—even a little baking soda can't change that.

southern sweet tea

MAKES 1 GALLON (3.8 L)
ACTIVE: 5 MINUTES
TOTAL: 50 MINUTES

6 family-size (7 g each) or 12 regular-size black tea bags

1 gallon (16 cups / 4 L) filtered or spring water, at room temperature, divided

½ teaspoon baking soda

1 to 1½ cups (200 to 300 g) granulated sugar

The best Southern sweet tea is made with a pinch of baking soda and Luzianne tea bags. Though this may raise some eyebrows, I prefer my tea on the less-sweet side, which is why I've provided a range for the amount of sugar. The sweetness level is up to you!

1. Place tea bags in a large glass jar or pitcher.
2. In a saucepan, bring 8 cups (2 L) of the water to a rolling boil over high heat; immediately pour over tea bags, making sure bags are submerged. Steep for 15 minutes. Remove bags and gently squeeze using kitchen tongs; discard bags.
3. Stir in baking soda and sugar until dissolved. Stir in remaining 8 cups (2 L) water. Refrigerate, uncovered, until chilled, about 30 minutes. Serve over ice. Store covered in refrigerator up to 2 days.

watermelon-basil sweet tea

SERVES 4
ACTIVE: 20 MINUTES
TOTAL: 1 HOUR, 40 MINUTES, INCLUDING SYRUP AND CHILLING

2 family-size or 6 regular tea bags

¼ cup (10 g) loosely packed fresh basil leaves

¼ teaspoon baking soda

5½ cups (1.3 L) water, divided

¾ cup (180 ml) Watermelon Simple Syrup, plus more if needed (page 60)

Basil sprigs, for garnish

Watermelon slices, for garnish

Use my Watermelon Simple Syrup on page 60 to make this delicious, summery twist on the Southern classic.

1. Place tea bags, basil leaves, and baking soda in a large glass jar or pitcher.
2. In a medium saucepan, bring 4 cups (960 ml) of the water to a rolling boil over high heat; immediately pour over tea bags and basil, making sure bags and leaves are submerged. Steep for 15 minutes. Remove basil and bags, gently squeezing them using kitchen tongs; discard bags and basil.
3. Stir in watermelon simple syrup and remaining 1½ cups (360 ml) water; add more simple syrup to taste, if desired.
4. Chill, uncovered, until cold, 1 to 2 hours. Serve over ice; garnish each serving with basil sprigs and watermelon slices. Store covered in refrigerator up to 2 days.

watermelon simple syrup

MAKES ABOUT 2⅓ CUPS (552 ML)
ACTIVE: 15 MINUTES
TOTAL: 1 HOUR

5 cups (1 pound, 10 ounces / 735 g) cubed seedless watermelon

1 cup (200 g) granulated sugar

Growing up, I spent many summer afternoons on our back porch eating watermelon, sticky juice dripping down my chin. Several years later, not much has changed. Inspired by one of our first *Southern Living* videos, this watermelon simple syrup infuses juicy watermelon flavor into three delicious drinks, all worthy of that sticky chin.

1. In a blender, process watermelon on medium-high speed until smooth, about 10 seconds. Pour through a fine mesh strainer into a medium bowl; discard solids. Measure out 2 cups (480 ml) juice; pour into a medium saucepan with granulated sugar. Reserve any remaining juice for another use.

2. Cook watermelon mixture over medium-high heat, stirring occasionally, until sugar is completely dissolved, about 5 minutes. Pour syrup into a medium heatproof bowl and let cool at room temperature for 45 minutes. Use immediately, or store in an airtight container in refrigerator up to 5 days.

watermelon frosé **(opposite)**

watermelon-basil sweet tea **(page 58)**

watermelon sangria **(opposite)**

watermelon sangria

SERVES 6
ACTIVE: 15 MINUTES
TOTAL: 45 MINUTES

1 (750-milliliter) bottle chilled Garnatxa Blanca or other dry, white Spanish wine

¾ cup (180 ml) Watermelon Simple Syrup (page 60)

1 cup (155 g) watermelon balls (from 1 small seedless watermelon)

4 medium fresh strawberries (3 ounces / 85 g total), trimmed and sliced

1 small peach (5 ounces / 140 g), sliced into 8 wedges

1 small lemon (3 ounces / 85 g), thinly sliced and seeded

Mint sprigs, for garnish

Place wine, watermelon simple syrup, watermelon balls, sliced strawberries, peach wedges, and lemon slices in a glass jar or pitcher; stir to combine. Chill, uncovered, for 30 minutes. Serve over ice. Garnish each serving with mint sprigs.

watermelon frosé

SERVES 8
ACTIVE: 5 MINUTES
TOTAL: 3 HOURS, 5 MINUTES

5 cups (1 pound, 5 ounces / 595 g) frozen watermelon chunks

1 (25-ounce / 750-ml) bottle chilled rosé (preferably from Pinot Noir grapes)

¾ cup (180 ml) Watermelon Simple Syrup (page 60), chilled

Fresh watermelon slices or spears, for garnish

In a blender, process watermelon, rosé, and watermelon simple syrup on medium-high speed until smooth, about 30 seconds. Pour watermelon mixture into a metal 9 by 13-inch (23 by 33-cm) baking pan. Freeze, covered, until mixture becomes icy and slushy, 3 to 4 hours. Spoon evenly into 8 glasses, and garnish with watermelon slices or spears. Serve immediately.

green chile lemonade

SERVES 6 TO 8
ACTIVE: 20 MINUTES
TOTAL: 2 HOURS, 20 MINUTES

3 cups (720 ml) water

1½ cups (360 ml) fresh lemon juice (from 8 to 10 lemons)

1½ cups (360 ml) Plain Simple Syrup (see page 54)

2 (4-ounce / 113-g) cans diced green chiles

Ice, for serving

Lemon wheels, for serving

Somewhere during the last week of September and the first week of October, you can usually find me in Hatch, New Mexico, with my friend Paige and her family. We visit the Hatch Valley to put up chile with her aunt and uncle who live there. If you've never visited New Mexico, it needs to be on your list—there is a reason they call it The Land of Enchantment. The famous Hatch green chiles are mostly known for enchiladas (like my Green Chile Chicken Enchiladas on page 139), cheeseburgers, or Rotel dip. But in New Mexico, they use them in almost everything. I've tried a lot of the popular green chile novelties, but my favorite by far is this lemonade. After a long day of "putting up" chiles, Paige and I love to go into town to Sparky's Burgers and BBQ for the spicy-tart treat. What used to be a once-a-year thing is now something I love to re-create at home when a hankering strikes—though nothing will ever beat Sparky's.

In a pitcher, stir water, lemon juice, simple syrup, and green chiles together. Chill at least 2 hours or up to overnight for maximum green chile flavor. Pour through a fine mesh strainer into a large measuring cup or another pitcher; discard green chiles. Serve over ice and garnish with lemon wheels.

ivy's take! When I drink green chile lemonade in New Mexico, the green chile is left in the glass, as opposed to straining it before it's served. For an authentic experience, I like to leave mine in when I'm making the spicy lemonade for myself. Though for a party, I recommend straining it, as the green chunks don't exactly look that delicious.

big-batch boozy arnold palmers

MAKES 13 CUPS (3 L)
ACTIVE: 10 MINUTES
TOTAL: 2 HOURS, 10 MINUTES

While regulated game play for the Masters Tournament doesn't technically start until Thursday of Masters Week, my festivities tee off on Wednesday, in time for the annual Par 3 Contest. Each day, I plan a special menu inspired by classic Masters fare, like pimiento cheese and Arnold Palmers. Even though the traditional drink doesn't contain alcohol, I make a spiked version for adults to sip on while they watch their favorite players. In true Ivy fashion, my recipe gets an extra punch from—you guessed it—bourbon. But, if vodka is more your speed, you've got yourself a John Daly, another great drink for a par-tee.

- 6 cups (1.4 L) prepared unsweetened tea
- 4 cups (960 ml) bottled lemonade
- 2¼ cups (18 ounces / 540 ml) bourbon
- ⅔ cup (165 ml) Plain Simple Syrup (page 54)
- 3 medium lemons, thinly sliced (about 24 slices)
- 12 mint sprigs, for garnish

In a large bowl or pitcher, stir together the tea, lemonade, bourbon, and simple syrup. Add lemon slices; refrigerate until chilled, at least 2 hours or overnight. Serve over ice, and garnish with mint sprigs and lemon slices.

azalea cocktail

SERVES 1
ACTIVE: 5 MINUTES
TOTAL: 5 MINUTES

The azalea is the signature drink served during the Masters at Augusta National. While the official version uses sweetened lemonade in place of plain lemon and pineapple juices, my preferred way to enjoy an azalea is this one.

- 2 ounces (60 ml) pineapple juice
- 2 ounces (60 ml) vodka
- 1 ounce (30 ml) fresh lemon juice
- 1 splash grenadine
- Lemon slice, for garnish

In a large glass or small pitcher, combine the pineapple juice, vodka, lemon juice, and grenadine. Add ice and stir. Strain mixture and pour over a glass filled with ice. Garnish with a lemon slice and serve immediately.

cucumber cooler

SERVES 1
ACTIVE: 10 MINUTES
TOTAL: 10 MINUTES

1½ pounds (680 g) cucumbers, cut into 1-inch pieces (about 3 large cucumbers)

½ cup (120 ml) tap water

2 tablespoons fresh lemon juice (from 1 large lemon)

2 tablespoons Plain Simple Syrup (page 54)

3 tablespoons (1½ ounces / 45 ml) gin, tequila, or vodka (optional)

Ice

Sparkling water

Lemon wheel, fresh mint, or basil, for garnish

One year when my garden was busting at the seams with cucumbers, I couldn't pickle them fast enough. To preserve my harvest, I threw some cucumbers, peel and all, in a blender and hoped for the best. The result was a delicious, refreshing juice that begged to be turned into a drink. After a hot day, this is just the thing I need to refuel. Booze is optional, though it may help convince a picky eater to try drinking their vegetables instead.

In a blender, process cucumbers and water until very smooth, about 2 minutes. Pour through a fine mesh strainer into a medium bowl or 3-cup (720-ml) container; discard solids. In a Collins glass, stir together ½ cup (120 ml) of the cucumber juice, lemon juice, simple syrup, and gin, as desired. Add ice and top with sparkling water. Garnish with lemon wheel and fresh herbs. (Reserve remaining cucumber juice for another use or store in an airtight container in freezer up to 6 months. Thaw completely before using.)

behind the scenes Use a mandolin to thinly slice cucumbers lengthwise to create cucumber "ribbons" to line your glass, pitcher, or dispenser for a pretty presentation. Just be extra careful when using a mandolin—they can be very dangerous!

chapter 3

what's for supper?

I think one thing any home cook will agree on is that we all don't look forward to getting asked the question, "What's for supper?" Before I got married, supper wasn't a major part of my day. My roommate, Paige, and I both worked in the *Southern Living* Test Kitchen. Oftentimes, we either ate too much at work to want supper, or we had leftovers from work we'd heat up, or we would just piece some semblance of a meal together out of this and that from our refrigerator. Supper was a loose term. It could be cheese and crackers, a small salad, or, on a "big" night, some sort of pasta. Though we aren't vegetarians, many nights would go by when there would be no meat on our plates, and it never bothered me. Fast forward a few years later when I started having Luis over for dinner, and I quickly learned supper could not be just cheese and crackers or pesto pasta. Supper needed to be a meat, WITH sides!

These days, supper is more of an undertaking than it used to be. I don't work in the test kitchens anymore, which means there aren't as many leftovers as there used to be. So, every Sunday, I find myself in the same place as many other home cooks—planning a week's worth of suppers with my husband. Once you figure out what to make, you then have to make a grocery list, go shopping, and, if you're really going for it, prep a few things ahead of time so that the upcoming weeknight meals will be a little easier.

So here's the deal: If I'm a professional cook who struggles this much with getting dinner on the table, I know that others struggle too. There are plenty of weeks that go by when I'm still dumbfounded as to what to prepare, which is when I turn to my arsenal of tried-and-true standbys. The recipes in this chapter are the ones I've made after a full day at the office. They're all about getting dinner on the table in under an hour, and in most cases, they have an active hands-on time of 30 minutes or less. We eat a lot of chicken thighs in our house, because not only are they the most delicious, juicy part of the bird, they cook relatively quickly. Many of our favorites are included here, but if you choose just one recipe to make, I would start with the Cold Skillet Crispy Chicken Thighs on page 70. There is also a "recipe" for when you don't feel like cooking at all on page 80, and a few veggie-forward ones that have even big carnivores—like Luis—calling a salad "supper." I hope some of the recipes on the pages that follow end up in your rotation so that the age-old question "What's for supper?" is at least a little bit easier to answer.

cold skillet crispy chicken thighs

SERVES 4
ACTIVE: 25 MINUTES
TOTAL: 45 MINUTES

4 bone-in, skin-on chicken thighs (2 pounds / 910 g)

1½ teaspoons kosher salt

If you make one recipe from this book, it should be this one. Don't get me wrong, I hope you love all the recipes here as much as I do. But this one is a real winner (chicken dinner). The thing I love most is that it's so stinking simple to make, and the result is so shockingly perfect that it's impossible not to love it. The technique, not the ingredients (literally just chicken and salt), is what makes this chicken incredible. By starting the chicken pieces skin side down in a cold skillet, you give the fat time to render slowly as it heats on the stove, which crisps the skin perfectly and flavors the chicken in a way no other cooking method can. When you cook the chicken completely in its own fat, it tastes more chicken-y (yes, that's an adjective). While it will work with skin-on chicken breasts if you increase the cooking time, I highly recommend making this with the thighs. Objectively, they are superior.

1. Preheat oven to 350°F (175°C). Pat chicken thighs very dry with paper towels, then sprinkle salt evenly over both sides of chicken.
2. Place thighs, skin side down, in a cold 10-inch (25-cm) cast-iron skillet, then place skillet over medium heat. Cook thighs over medium heat until skin is golden and crisp, about 15 minutes. Be sure to be attentive to any hot spots, moving the skillet and thighs around to avoid over-browning.
3. When chicken skin is golden and crisp, flip thighs in skillet, being sure to fold any excess skin under the thighs to keep crisping. Transfer skillet to preheated oven and cook until a thermometer inserted in the thickest portion of the thigh registers 160°F (71°C), 8 to 10 more minutes. Remove chicken from oven and transfer to a plate to rest for 10 minutes before serving. (Chicken will continue to cook while resting to reach an internal temperature of 165°F / 74°C.) If desired, spoon any residual pan drippings over chicken before serving.

serving tip: Serve this with a fork and knife or on a sandwich with Hot Honey Mustard (page 27) or Goes-on-Everything Balsamic Syrup (page 26). It would also be great with Summer Pasta (page 90) or on top of Ivy's Famous Caesar Salad (page 83).

weeknight fried chicken

SERVES 6
ACTIVE: 40 MINUTES
TOTAL: 40 MINUTES

⅓ cup (40 g) all-purpose flour

1 tablespoon House Seasoning (page 20), divided

1½ cups (120 g) panko breadcrumbs

1 teaspoon kosher salt, divided

2 large eggs

6 boneless skinless chicken thighs (1¼ pounds / 567 g)

Extra-virgin olive oil, for frying

Crispy chicken (cutlets, thighs, or fingers) is frequently in my dinner rotation. They're a great protein for when you've got most of the rest of the meal taken care of, like salad or leftover veggies and a starch from the night before. I don't love cooking these when I have to deal with too many other components, because while they are very easy, they do take the full amount of hands-on time. When I'm making dinner, I prefer to have only one active, stovetop part of the meal, so that I don't have too many things going on at once. If I'm busy at the stove with a protein, sides need to be fully in the oven or leftover and reheated, and vice versa. Getting supper on the table shouldn't be more stressful than it needs to be. Trust me, even I stress about suppertime. My biggest piece of advice? Know when it's just better to run to Chick-fil-A.

1. Gather three shallow bowls or pie dishes. Place flour into one shallow bowl with 1 teaspoon house seasoning; whisk to combine. Place panko in second shallow bowl with 1 teaspoon house seasoning and ½ teaspoon salt; whisk to combine. Crack eggs into the third shallow bowl. Add remaining 1 teaspoon house seasoning and remaining ½ teaspoon salt to eggs and beat well with a whisk.

2. Line a baking sheet with paper towels. Open up chicken thighs to one flat layer. (Grocery stores will usually package boneless skinless chicken thighs folded up, so be sure to unfold.) Working with 1 chicken thigh at a time, dredge the thigh in the flour mixture first, being sure to coat all sides. Next, dredge the thigh in the egg mixture, coating well, but allowing any excess to drip off before finally dredging thigh in panko mixture. Press panko mixture into the chicken thigh to adhere. Place breaded thigh on paper towel–lined baking sheet. Continue dredging remaining thighs in this order until all are breaded.

3. Pour enough olive oil into a large nonstick skillet to cover the bottom fully, about ⅓ cup (75 ml). Heat oil over medium heat. To test if the oil is hot, drop a pinch of panko dredging into the oil. When oil is hot, the panko will sizzle and float instead of sinking to the bottom. Working in two batches, fry thighs 4 to 5 minutes per side, or until golden brown, crisp, and a thermometer inserted into the thickest portion of the thigh registers 165°F (74°C). Adjust heat to prevent over-browning. Let cooked chicken drain on a paper towel–lined plate until ready to serve. Add more oil to the skillet and allow to heat before frying remaining chicken thighs. Allow chicken to rest 5 minutes before slicing to serve.

oven-baked chicken thighs with vegetables

SERVES 4
ACTIVE: 25 MINUTES
TOTAL: 40 MINUTES

4 tablespoons (60 ml) olive oil, divided

4 (6-ounce / 170-g) bone-in, skin-on chicken thighs

2½ teaspoons kosher salt, divided

1 teaspoon freshly ground black pepper, divided

2 medium lemons, halved

¼ cup (60 ml) water

2 medium sweet potatoes, cut into 3-inch (7.5-cm) wedges (4 cups / 228 g)

3 cups (12 ounces / 340 g) Brussels sprouts, trimmed and halved

2 large shallots, halved

1 large garlic clove, grated (1 teaspoon)

1 tablespoon whole-grain mustard

1 teaspoon honey

1 teaspoon Worcestershire sauce

1 teaspoon chopped fresh rosemary

Rosemary sprigs

The best part about this meal is it uses one skillet. Anything that saves on cleanup time always gets extra points in my book. Switch up the veggies for whatever you have on hand. Broccoli, carrots, green beans, or butternut squash would all be delicious!

1. Preheat oven to 400°F (205°C) with oven rack in bottom third of oven. In a large cast-iron skillet, heat 1 tablespoon of the oil on stovetop over medium-high heat. Pat chicken dry with a paper towel; sprinkle evenly with 1½ teaspoons of the salt and ½ teaspoon of the pepper.

2. Place chicken, skin side down, in hot oil. Add lemon halves, cut sides down, to skillet. Cook until chicken skin is golden and crisp and lemons are charred, 8 to 10 minutes. Transfer lemons to a rimmed baking sheet. Flip chicken, and continue cooking until golden on both sides, 4 to 5 minutes. Transfer chicken to baking sheet with lemons. Pour drippings from skillet into a small bowl and reserve. Add water to skillet and stir to loosen browned bits on bottom with a wooden spoon. Discard liquid; wipe skillet clean.

3. Heat remaining 3 tablespoons of oil in skillet over medium-high heat. Add sweet potatoes and cook for 2 minutes. Add Brussels sprouts and shallots to skillet. Sprinkle vegetables with remaining 1 teaspoon salt. Cook until charred, about 5 minutes. Remove skillet from heat.

4. Add grated garlic, whole-grain mustard, honey, Worcestershire sauce, and juice of 2 of the charred lemon halves (about 1 tablespoon) to reserved drippings in bowl, and whisk to combine. Return charred lemon halves (including squeezed lemon halves) to skillet with vegetables. Place chicken, skin side up, on top. Pour the drippings mixture evenly over chicken.

5. Place skillet in preheated oven and bake until vegetables are tender and a thermometer inserted into thickest portion of chicken registers 160°F (71°C), 15 to 18 minutes. Remove from oven and let stand 10 minutes (chicken temperature should rise to 165°F / 74°C). Sprinkle with chopped rosemary and remaining ½ teaspoon pepper. Garnish with rosemary sprigs.

grilled chicken salad with pickled blueberries

SERVES 4
ACTIVE: 35 MINUTES
TOTAL: 40 MINUTES

1 cup (240 ml) red wine vinegar

½ cup (110 g) packed light brown sugar

3 whole cloves

1 tablespoon, plus 1½ teaspoons kosher salt, divided

1 small red onion, thinly sliced (1½ cups / 165 g)

1 (6-ounce / 170-g) package fresh blueberries

½ teaspoon freshly ground black pepper

7 tablespoons (105 ml) olive oil, divided

4 (8-ounce / 225-g) boneless, skinless chicken breasts

1 teaspoon Dijon mustard

½ teaspoon fresh lemon juice (from 1 lemon)

8 ounces (225 g) spring mix salad greens

8 ounces (2 cups / 225 g) goat cheese, crumbled

1 cup (100 g) candied pecans

Pickled blueberries might be your new favorite salad topper. You could easily leave the onions out of the pickling liquid for a sweet, tangy treat that would be great on vanilla ice cream! I often make this salad with leftover cooked chicken, which cuts the total time in half. But if you do find yourself needing to cook chicken, this simple grilled breast is a tasty way to do it.

1. In a medium saucepan, whisk together vinegar, sugar, cloves, and 1 tablespoon of the salt. Bring to a boil over medium-high heat. Continue boiling, stirring occasionally, until sugar and salt dissolve, about 5 minutes. Place onion slices and blueberries in a medium heatproof bowl and pour hot vinegar mixture over onion and blueberries. Let cool completely to room temperature, about 30 minutes.

2. Meanwhile, in a small bowl, stir together pepper, 2 tablespoons of the oil, and remaining 1½ teaspoons salt. Brush mixture evenly over chicken breasts. Preheat a gas grill to medium-high (400° to 450°F / 205° to 230°C). Place chicken on unoiled grates. Grill, uncovered, until a thermometer inserted in thickest portion of meat registers 155°F (68°C), 7 to 8 minutes per side. Transfer chicken to a cutting board and rest for 10 minutes. (Chicken will continue to cook while resting to reach an internal temperature of 165°F/74°C.) Cut into ¾-inch (2-cm) slices.

3. Measure 3 tablespoons pickling liquid into a medium bowl. Add mustard, lemon juice, and remaining 5 tablespoons oil; whisk until smooth. Place salad greens in a large bowl, add mustard mixture, goat cheese, and pecans. Toss to coat. Drain remaining pickling liquid from onion and blueberries; discard liquid and cloves. Add onion and blueberries to salad; toss to combine. Divide evenly among four bowls; top with sliced chicken.

ivy's take! If you can't tell by the number of pickle or pickle-flavored recipes in this book, I'm a big fan of pickling. While I do draw the line at pickled pigs' feet, there isn't much that I wouldn't eat as a pickle. For me, one of the best things about pickles is actually the pickle juice. It's jam-packed with flavor that deserves a second life beyond the pickle jar. My recipes for Not Your Mama's Broccoli Salad (page 153), Party Potato Salad (page 149), Classic Deviled Eggs (page 165), and this recipe for Grilled Chicken Salad with Pickled Blueberries all call for pickling liquid to add a surprising zingy boost.

no-recipe-needed
chicken wraps (page 80)

tomato, cucumber, and onion salad (page 81)

no-recipe-needed chicken wraps

TYPICALLY SERVES 4
ACTIVE: 15 MINUTES
TOTAL: 15 MINUTES

Cooked chicken, sliced or shredded, such as rotisserie or leftover Sunday Roasted Chicken (page 224)

Naan bread, grilled, charred, or heated in the microwave with a damp paper towel

Tomato, Cucumber, and Onion Salad (page 81)

Store-bought hummus of choice

Store-bought tzatziki sauce

Fresh dill sprigs

Za'atar seasoning, or a blend of Mediterranean-inspired herbs and spices

Feta, crumbled

Lettuce leaves or spring mix

Pickled Onions (page 210)

When I don't feel like cooking, this is what I make for supper. It takes about 15 minutes to pull everything together, and everyone fixes their own plates. I set it out, pour myself a glass of wine, and enjoy a fuss-free meal. The best part about it? No recipe required! Just set out some or all of these suggested components, or add some of your own, and let everyone get creative!

1. Heat up your chicken (or serve it cold), and set the rest of the components on the table or counter. Have everyone fix their own plates the way they like them while you sit back and enjoy not cooking.

2. I like to spread hummus and tzatziki on my pita before adding chicken, veggies, and the rest of the toppings, then I eat it like a wrap or gyro. You might prefer to eat this more like a bowl or salad, with the naan on the side. That's the beauty of letting everyone choose their own adventure. One less thing you have to decide—we make enough decisions all day as it is.

tomato, cucumber, and onion salad

MAKES 4 CUPS (720 G)
ACTIVE: 10 MINUTES
TOTAL: 25 MINUTES

2 medium tomatoes, cut into 1-inch (2.5-cm) pieces, or 12 ounces (340 g) cherry or grape tomatoes, halved

1 (12-ounce / 340-g) English cucumber, cut into 1-inch (2.5-cm) pieces

1 small sweet onion, thinly sliced (1¼ cups / 140 g)

¼ cup (60 ml) extra-virgin olive oil

2 tablespoons vinegar of choice (balsamic, sherry, rice, red wine, or white wine vinegar)

1½ teaspoons kosher salt

½ teaspoon freshly ground black pepper

½ cup (25 g) torn soft herbs of choice (basil, dill, parsley, mint, or cilantro)

Flaky sea salt, such as Maldon, for serving

I make a variation of this recipe at least twice a week during the summer. By switching up the vinegar, herbs—and sometimes the oil—I never get tired of eating dressed tomatoes, cucumbers, and onions. You can add one or all of the herbs to really bring out the flavor. If I use rice vinegar, I like to add in a little toasted sesame oil and some chopped peanuts for a fun Thai-inspired twist. If you find the vinegar a little too acidic, you can always add in just a touch of honey.

I love to use any leftover juices in the bowl to spoon over the rest of my plate or as the start to a salad dressing. Sometimes I also just slurp up the juices straight from the bowl! See page 28 for my favorite salad dressing recipe—a great use for stirring in the leftover juices.

In a medium bowl, toss together tomatoes, cucumber, onion, oil, vinegar, salt, and pepper. Let stand at room temperature for 15 minutes. Toss in herbs just before serving; garnish with flaky sea salt.

behind the scenes When I worked in the test kitchens, we often had lots of food set out on counters to scavenge for lunch. Whether the recipes were being developed for the first time, tested for accuracy, or being photographed for publication, we could usually count on finding someone's leftovers to make do. But on the occasional day that the only thing coming out of anyone's kitchen was a layer cake or pie, I would make Caesar salad. As delicious as the desserts were, they didn't make for the healthiest lunches. Word would quickly spread down the hallway that I was taking my croutons out of the oven, and within minutes everyone would flock to my kitchen counter.

ivy's famous caesar salad with homemade croutons

SERVES 8 (MAKES 1⅓ CUPS / 315 ML DRESSING)
ACTIVE: 30 MINUTES
TOTAL: 1 HOUR, INCLUDING CROUTONS

This Caesar dressing is creamy and garlicky, and it clings to the romaine like it should. But the real star of the show is the croutons. If you don't keep an eye on them, they might get eaten up before they even make it to the salad bowl.

3 large egg yolks

½ cup (120 ml) extra-virgin olive oil

1 tablespoon Worcestershire sauce

2 teaspoons red wine vinegar

2 teaspoons fresh lemon juice (from 1 lemon)

1 teaspoon kosher salt

1 teaspoon freshly grated black pepper, plus more for garnish

½ teaspoon grated garlic (from 1 large clove)

2 anchovy fillets, finely chopped into a paste (½ teaspoon paste)

⅔ cup (65 g) grated Parmesan cheese

1 tablespoon water

12 cups (660 g) chopped romaine lettuce (from 2 hearts of romaine)

3 cups (120 g) Homemade Croutons (opposite), divided

½ cup (50 g) shaved Parmesan cheese

1 In a medium bowl, lightly beat egg yolks with a whisk. Slowly drizzle oil into egg yolks, whisking constantly. Yolks and oil should emulsify and thicken, almost to the consistency of mayonnaise. Once all oil is whisked in and mixture is thick, whisk in Worcestershire, vinegar, lemon juice, salt, pepper, garlic, and anchovies. Whisk in grated Parmesan and water until smooth.

2 Place romaine in a large serving bowl. Drizzle Caesar dressing over romaine and add in half of the croutons. Toss to coat. Garnish salad with shaved Parmesan, remaining half of croutons, and freshly grated black pepper. Serve immediately.

homemade croutons

MAKES ABOUT 5 CUPS (200 G)

6 slices (10 ounces / 280 g) thick-sliced soft white sandwich bread, such as Sara Lee Artesano, cut into ¾-inch (2-cm) cubes (½ loaf of Sara Lee Artesano)

6 tablespoons (85 g) salted butter

4 large garlic cloves, smashed

½ teaspoon kosher salt

1 Preheat oven to 350°F (175°C) and line a rimmed baking sheet with parchment paper. Spread bread cubes in an even layer on baking sheet.

2 Place butter and garlic cloves in a microwave-safe measuring cup. Microwave, stirring every 20 seconds, until butter is melted, 1 minute to 1 minute 20 seconds. Pour butter mixture evenly over bread cubes. Gently toss to coat bread cubes in butter. Season with salt; toss gently. Bake in preheated oven until golden brown and crisp on the outside and slightly soft on the inside, about 20 minutes. Let cool completely before serving. Store in an airtight container up to 5 days.

blackened fish-of-the-day sandwich

SERVES 4
ACTIVE: 30 MINUTES
TOTAL: 30 MINUTES, INCLUDING SEASONING AND SAUCE

4 (5 to 5½-ounce / 140 to 155-g) mild, flaky white fish fillets, such as grouper, snapper, redfish, etc.

6 teaspoons Blackened Seasoning (recipe follows)

4 tablespoons (55 g) salted butter, divided

4 brioche-style hamburger buns

6 tablespoons (90 ml) Tartar Ranch (recipe follows)

1 beefsteak tomato, thinly sliced

Kosher salt

8 butter, romaine, or green leaf lettuce leaves

I don't make it down to the gulf as much anymore as I did when I was younger. Thanks to my parents, I practically grew up on Saint George Island, Florida. On the days when I long for the salt water, I head over to my local fishmonger and ask for his freshest catch, usually grouper, snapper, or redfish, and I make this sandwich. It may not be as good as one you'd eat at a salt-air-breeze-filled beach bar, but it's pretty close.

1 Pat fish fillets dry on all sides with paper towels. Season all sides of each fillet with 1½ teaspoons of the Blackened Seasoning.

2 In a large nonstick skillet, heat 2 tablespoons of the butter over medium heat. Place buns, cut side down, in skillet, swirling around in skillet so they absorb the melted butter. Cook until buns are lightly toasted, about 4 minutes. Remove buns from skillet and set aside.

3 In skillet, heat 1 tablespoon of remaining butter over medium heat until melted, swirling to coat the surface. Place fillets in skillet and cook for 5 minutes on the first side. (Note: I prefer my fillets on the thicker side, about ¾ to 1 inch / 2 to 2.5 cm thick, but if your fillets are thinner, flip after about 4 minutes.) Continue cooking on the second side 4 to 5 more minutes, or longer for thicker fillets. Add remaining 1 tablespoon butter to skillet; let butter melt. With the skillet still on the heat, carefully tilt skillet toward you, so the butter pools in the bottom front of skillet. Spoon melted butter over the fillets, allowing butter to melt over the fillets and pool back in the skillet again. Continue basting fillets with the butter for 1 to 2 minutes, or until fish flakes easily with a fork. Transfer fillets to a plate to rest while you assemble the sandwiches.

4 Spread bottoms and tops of toasted bun halves with Tartar Ranch (each sandwich should get about 1½ tablespoons). Top each bottom bun half with 1 fillet, 1 to 2 tomato slices, salt to taste, and 2 lettuce leaves; top with top halves of buns. Serve immediately.

blackened seasoning

MAKES 5 TABLESPOONS

- 5 teaspoons smoked paprika
- 1 tablespoon garlic powder
- 1 tablespoon Italian seasoning
- 2½ teaspoons kosher salt
- 2 teaspoons onion powder
- 1 teaspoon freshly ground black pepper
- ½ teaspoon cayenne pepper
- ½ teaspoon celery salt

In a small bowl, stir together all ingredients. Store in an airtight container at room temperature up to 6 months.

tartar ranch

MAKES ABOUT ⅔ CUP (165 ML)

- ½ cup (120 ml) mayonnaise
- 1 teaspoon Dijon mustard
- 1 tablespoon finely chopped dill pickle
- 1 tablespoon chopped fresh dill
- 1 teaspoon grated sweet onion (from 1 small onion)
- 1 teaspoon fresh lemon juice (from 1 lemon)
- ½ teaspoon Worcestershire sauce
- ¼ teaspoon freshly ground black pepper
- 1 teaspoon drained capers, smashed into a paste (optional)

In a small bowl, stir together all ingredients until well-combined. Serve immediately or store in an airtight container in the refrigerator up to 3 days.

pineapple-pepper slaw

SERVES 8
ACTIVE: 15 MINUTES
TOTAL: 25 MINUTES

4 cups (380 g) shredded green cabbage (from 1 head)

2 cups (190 g) shredded red cabbage (from 1 small head)

2 cups (170 g) small cubes fresh pineapple

1 medium red bell pepper, thinly sliced

½ cup (20 g) loosely packed fresh cilantro leaves

½ cup (30 g) thinly sliced green onions (from 2 green onions)

2 tablespoons minced seeded jalapeño chile (from 1 jalapeño)

1 teaspoon lime zest plus 2 tablespoons fresh juice (from 2 limes)

1 teaspoon honey

1 teaspoon kosher salt

¼ teaspoon freshly ground black pepper

⅓ cup (75 ml) extra-virgin olive oil

I grew up on the classic, sweet, mayonnaise-based coleslaws traditionally served with a basket of fried catfish and hush puppies. I love that kind of slaw, and so do my parents. It wasn't until later on I learned to love oil-and-vinegar-dressed slaws. The first time I made one for my dad, I remember him saying, "This is good, but this is not slaw." Mama agreed with him. After a few trial-and-error attempts at getting them to hop on board, this recipe is what I landed on. It's great as a flavorful side, but even better as a crunchy topping for a fish taco or chicken sandwich.

1 In a large bowl, toss together green cabbage, red cabbage, pineapple, bell pepper, cilantro, green onions, and jalapeño.

2 In a small bowl, whisk together lime zest and juice, honey, salt, and pepper. Add oil in a slow, steady stream, whisking constantly until smooth. Add vinaigrette to cabbage mixture; toss to coat. Let stand 10 minutes, toss again, and serve.

behind the scenes When we first set out to film *Hey Y'all*, we went all out on our episode ideas. The first two episodes were shot over the course of two very adventurous days: one spent fishing and playing with baby pigs and the other totally transforming my home kitchen into a video set. For the fishing episode, I talked about how fishing, particularly for catfish, is such a Southern pastime. I showed people how to fry catfish in a crispy cornmeal batter (see page 229), but instead of serving it with the traditional cheese grits and hushpuppies, I made fish tacos topped with this Pineapple-Pepper Slaw. Tangy, sweet, and perfectly crunchy, it's great with fried fish or on my fish sandwiches (see page 84).

Disclaimer: This story involves two people named Rebecca. Rebecca Lang, who you can read more about on page 221, is a cookbook author, cooking instructor, and television personality who lives in Athens, Georgia. She is my mentor and one of my very dear friends. Rebecca Rykard Lovett has been my best friend since the tenth grade. We went to the University of Georgia together, and though we now live in separate cities and don't get to see each other nearly as often as we should, when we do, we pick up right where we left off, which is always the summer of 2015.

There will never be a summer that is better than that one. I was living in Athens, Georgia, finishing up a few classes and working for Rebecca Lang on her sixth cookbook, the second one I'd had the privilege of helping her with. Between recipe testing, traveling for cooking demos, and my four classes, I always had something to do. On my free nights, my best friend (the other Rebecca) would come over for supper. We cooked so many delicious meals together and enjoyed them all with a glass of rosé on my back patio. There was fresh creamed corn, roasted pork tenderloin, and a LOT of pasta. We invented a dish that we called Our Pasta. It was spaghetti tossed in a garlicky olive oil sauce with burst cherry tomatoes, feta, Parmesan, fresh basil, and bread crumbs. At the time, we thought it was the best thing ever, and it was.

But when I think back on that recipe, I cringe. With all of the cooking knowledge I've gained since then, there are a lot of things I would do now to make Our Pasta even better. I'd save the pasta water, for one. And I'd take out the feta—those briny curds just don't go. I'd also top the final dish with some crispy bread crumbs instead of tossing them in the noodles during the last bit of cooking. (What was I thinking?!) Enter: Summer Pasta (page 90). This recipe takes everything we loved about Our Pasta and only makes it better. The sauce is glossier (thanks to that pasta water), the bread crumbs are actually crispy, and there's even some rosé and fresh corn in there as a nod to our other most-consumed food groups from The Best Summer Ever! It's one of my absolute favorite recipes in this book, not just because it's really stinking delicious, but because it reminds me of my best friend, and the summer of suppers I'll never forget.

summer pasta

SERVES 6
ACTIVE: 30 MINUTES
TOTAL: 30 MINUTES

2 tablespoons extra-virgin olive oil

¾ cup (60 g) panko bread crumbs

2 teaspoons very thinly sliced basil leaves

½ teaspoon lemon zest (from 1 lemon)

1½ teaspoons kosher salt plus ¼ cup (60 g), divided

12 cups (2.8 L) water

½ cup (110 g) unsalted butter, divided

1 cup (110 g) chopped sweet onion (from 1 small onion)

12 ounces (340 g) bucatini

1 pint (290 g) multicolored cherry tomatoes, halved

1½ cups (220 g) corn kernels, from 2 ears (any color corn will do)

1 tablespoon minced garlic (from 2 large cloves)

½ teaspoon crushed red pepper

⅓ cup (75 ml) dry white wine

½ cup (120 ml) heavy cream

2 teaspoons fresh lemon juice (from 1 lemon)

1 cup (100 g) freshly grated Parmesan cheese

Freshly ground black pepper, for garnish

Basil leaves, for garnish

Never, and I mean never, throw out your pasta cooking water until you're completely done cooking. I've even been known to save it in the fridge to add a little to reheated leftovers. The starchy water is key to creating a glossy sauce that coats pasta perfectly.

1. In a 12-inch (30.5 cm) nonstick skillet, heat oil over medium heat. Add panko and cook, stirring often, until panko is golden brown, about 7 minutes. Remove from heat and stir in basil, lemon zest, and ½ teaspoon of the salt. Transfer to a small bowl, then wipe skillet clean.

2. In a large pot, bring water and ¼ cup (60 g) of the salt to a boil over high heat. While water is coming up to a boil, add ¼ cup (55 g) of the butter to the same nonstick skillet and cook over medium-high heat until just melted. Add onion to skillet and cook, stirring occasionally, until soft, about 6 minutes. When water starts to boil, add bucatini to pot and cook until al dente, about 7 minutes. Use a ladle to reserve 1 cup (240 ml) pasta water in a measuring cup, then drain pasta.

3. Once the onions are soft, add tomatoes and corn to the skillet and cook, stirring occasionally, until tomatoes begin to burst, 3 to 4 minutes. Stir in garlic and crushed red pepper and cook over medium heat, stirring constantly, until fragrant, about 1 minute. Stir in white wine and cook until liquid reduces by half and alcohol smell has dissipated, about 2 minutes.

4. Add remaining ¼ cup (55 g) butter to skillet and cook until just melted, then stir in heavy cream, remaining 1 teaspoon salt, and half of the reserved pasta water. Add pasta to skillet and cook, tossing constantly with tongs while slowly adding in remaining half of the pasta water, until glossy. Add lemon juice and Parmesan to pasta, tossing until just incorporated. Transfer pasta to a serving platter and garnish with freshly ground black pepper and basil leaves, then top with panko mixture to serve.

Basil Smash
lemon
basil
agave
gin or bourbon
Nana's Kitchen
Tea Cakes

mama's caramelized squash

SERVES 4
ACTIVE: 35 MINUTES
TOTAL: 35 MINUTES

2 tablespoons extra-virgin olive oil, butter, or bacon grease

2 pounds (910 g) yellow squash, cut into ¼-inch (6 mm) slices

1 cup (110 g) chopped sweet onion (from 1 small onion)

2 tablespoons water

1¼ teaspoons kosher salt

½ teaspoon freshly ground black pepper

Fresh thyme sprigs, for garnish

Also known as "squash 'n' onions," this is one of my very favorite side dishes my mama made for supper during my childhood. She had a lot of sides she called "veggies 'n' onions" (see Mama's Potatoes and Onions on page 97), cooked exactly like these, in a cast-iron skillet, usually with bacon grease. On the rare occasions we were out of that liquid gold, she'd use oil or butter, which are almost as delicious.

1 In a 12-inch (30.5 cm) cast-iron skillet, heat oil, butter, or bacon grease over medium heat until melted. Add squash and onions to skillet and cook, stirring occasionally, until onions and squash are tender and begin to turn golden brown, 15 to 17 minutes.

2 Add 2 tablespoons water to skillet and continue cooking until onions are completely caramelized and squash is browned in some spots, 10 to 15 more minutes. Season with salt and pepper, then remove from heat. Garnish with fresh thyme before serving.

if this isn't southern . . . In the South, cast-iron skillets are passed down through the generations with the same reverence as heirloom jewelry. In fact for some, the skillets might be of more sentimental value. When we moved my nana out of her house of sixty years and into an apartment, my mama kept most of her skillets, saying that I'd get them when it was my turn. I got two out of Nana's collection that I cook with almost every day. They're the most well-seasoned skillets in my arsenal. I swear, everything I cook in them just tastes better because it touched Nana's skillet. I'll pass them down, along with the ones I'll get from Mama, eventually. And I hope that future generations will know the skillets, and the memories they'll make using them, are far more precious than gold.

roasted smashed potatoes

SERVES 4
ACTIVE: 10 MINUTES
TOTAL: 55 MINUTES

1½ pounds (680 g) baby red potatoes

2 tablespoons olive oil

2 teaspoons House Seasoning (page 20)

When I have a little extra time to get supper on the table, I love to make these potatoes. They aren't difficult, they just take a while to roast to reach maximum crispiness. You could easily parboil the potatoes instead of roasting them, but I've found they turn out more flavorful and crispier if you roast them twice. They're the perfect side to any protein, especially when served with my Shortcut Garlic Aioli (page 25).

1 Preheat oven to 425°F (220°C). Line a rimmed baking sheet with parchment paper or aluminum foil. Place potatoes in a single layer on baking sheet and bake in preheated oven for 20 minutes, or until tender.

2 Remove baking sheet from oven. Use a heatproof bowl, cup, jar, or measuring cup to smash potatoes until they are about ½ inch (12 mm) thick. Drizzle potatoes evenly with oil, then sprinkle evenly with House Seasoning. Carefully spread potatoes apart as best as you can so they are in a single layer without touching. Return baking sheet to oven and continue baking for another 20 to 25 minutes, until potatoes are golden brown and crisp. Serve immediately.

browned butter mashed potatoes

SERVES 6
ACTIVE: 30 MINUTES
TOTAL: 30 MINUTES

2½ pounds (1.2 kg) Yukon Gold potatoes, peeled and cut into 2-inch (5-cm) pieces

1 tablespoon unsalted butter

1 teaspoon very finely chopped fresh garlic

⅓ cup (75 ml) heavy whipping cream

2 teaspoons kosher salt

¾ cup (180 ml) Browned Butter (page 23), melted and divided

If you want to impress everyone at the table, brown your butter before mixing it into your mashed potatoes. I promise you'll get oohs and aahs. While I love to make this for a fancy date night in, it's also one of my go-to sides to bring with a meal for new parents who need a little boost.

1 Place potatoes in a medium saucepan with just enough water to fully submerge. Bring to a boil over medium-high heat and cook until potatoes are tender, about 20 minutes. Meanwhile, in a small saucepan, melt unsalted butter over medium heat. Add garlic and cook until fragrant, about 1 minute, being careful not to let it burn. Add in cream, reduce heat to low, and let cream heat while potatoes finish cooking. When potatoes are tender, drain and return potatoes to saucepan.

2 Heat potatoes in saucepan over medium heat and cook, stirring occasionally, to cook any excess water off the potatoes, about 1 minute. Add hot cream mixture and mash with a potato masher until cream is just incorporated, but mixture is still chunky. Stir in salt and ½ cup (120 ml) of the melted browned butter, continuing to mash until potatoes are smooth. Transfer potatoes to a serving bowl; spoon remaining melted browned butter over the potatoes just before serving.

mama's potatoes and onions

SERVES 4
ACTIVE: 40 MINUTES
TOTAL: 40 MINUTES

¼ cup (60 ml) bacon grease

2 tablespoons canola oil

1½ pounds (680 g) russet potatoes (about 3 medium potatoes), peeled and cut into ¾-inch (2-cm) chunks

1½ cups (165 g) chopped sweet onion (from 1 medium onion)

2 teaspoons kosher salt

½ teaspoon garlic powder

¼ teaspoon freshly ground black pepper

My mama taught me how to make a lot of things, but this is by far my favorite. It's a humble side dish that I'd be willing to bet every Southerner has fond memories of. For me, it's love in a cast-iron skillet.

1. In a 12-inch (30.5 cm) cast-iron skillet, heat bacon grease and oil over medium-high heat until melted. Add potatoes and toss until coated.
2. Cover and cook, undisturbed, for 5 minutes, or until a few potatoes have browned slightly. Add onions, salt, garlic powder, and pepper; stir to combine. Reduce the heat to medium and cook, uncovered and stirring occasionally, until potatoes are tender on the inside and browned on the outside, 15 to 20 minutes longer. Be careful not to stir too much, as this will prevent browning. It is okay if some of the potatoes get dark spots—this adds to the caramelized flavor.

collard green salad with shallot-sherry vinaigrette

SERVES 6
ACTIVE: 20 MINUTES
TOTAL: 20 MINUTES

8 cups (440 g) very thinly sliced or shredded collard greens (stems removed)

½ cup (120 ml) Shallot-Sherry Vinaigrette, divided (recipe follows)

¼ teaspoon kosher salt

2 medium carrots, peeled and shaved into ribbons with a vegetable peeler (¾ cup / 85 g ribbons)

1 small Honeycrisp apple, very thinly sliced

⅓ cup (45 g) sweetened dried cranberries

½ cup (60 g) chopped candied pecans

2 tangerines, Cara Cara oranges, or Minneola tangelos, peeled and segmented or sliced

2 ounces (55 g) goat cheese, crumbled

I debated naming this recipe Oh No! My Book Is Too Brown, I Need A Salad! because that is partly why it ended up here. I do love a salad, especially this one in the fall, but when you're trying to narrow down your all-time favorite recipes to include in a cookbook, you don't think about the lack of color the recipes display. After sending a full batch of all-brown recipes through the test kitchens for cross-testing, I immediately added this to the mix. I'm so glad I did, and not just for the color—it really is delightful.

1. In a large bowl, place collards with ¼ cup (60 ml) of the Shallot-Sherry Vinaigrette and salt. Use your hands to massage dressing into collards to tenderize, about 1 minute. Add carrot ribbons, apple slices, dried cranberries, and remaining Shallot-Sherry Vinaigrette to bowl; toss well to coat.

2. Transfer salad to a serving bowl or platter; top with candied pecans, citrus segments, and goat cheese. Serve immediately.

shallot-sherry vinaigrette

MAKES ABOUT ½ CUP (120 ML)

2 tablespoons sherry vinegar (or apple cider vinegar)

1 tablespoon Dijon mustard

1 tablespoon honey

5 tablespoons (75 ml) extra-virgin olive oil

2 tablespoons finely chopped shallot (from 1 small shallot)

¼ teaspoon kosher salt

In a medium bowl, whisk together vinegar, mustard, and honey until smooth. Slowly whisk in olive oil until emulsified, then stir in shallot and salt. Use immediately or refrigerate until ready to use, up to 2 days.

cast-iron skillet ribeyes with mushroom pan sauce

SERVES 2 TO 4 (DEPENDING ON HOW HUNGRY YOU ARE)
ACTIVE: 25 MINUTES
TOTAL: 55 MINUTES

2 bone-in rib eyes, at least ¾-inch (2-cm) thick (1 to 1½ pounds / 455 to 680 g each)

2¼ teaspoons kosher salt, divided

1 tablespoon canola oil

6 tablespoons (85 g) unsalted butter, chilled, divided

3 large garlic cloves, smashed

4 sprigs fresh thyme

8 ounces (3 cups / 225 g) baby bella mushrooms, sliced ¼-inch (6-mm) thick

2 teaspoons minced garlic (from 2 medium cloves)

⅔ cup (165 ml) dry red wine

1 teaspoon Worcestershire sauce

½ teaspoon freshly ground black pepper

Flaky salt, for serving

I grew up on grilled steaks, and even to this day when I go home to visit my parents, my dad insists on firing up the grill for our steak dinners. I love the flavor grilling creates, but when I tried a perfectly seared cast-iron skillet ribeye, I knew I would never even bother learning how to properly grill one. Once you cook a steak in a cast-iron skillet, you'll never do it any other way ever again.

1 Season each ribeye with 1 teaspoon salt (½ teaspoon salt per side). Lay ribeyes on paper towels and let sit at room temperature at least 30 minutes or up to 1 hour before cooking. Meanwhile, preheat oven to 400°F (205°C).

2 Heat a 12-inch (30.5 cm) cast-iron skillet over high heat for 5 minutes. Pat ribeyes very dry with paper towels. Add oil and just as oil begins to smoke, place 1 of the steaks into hot skillet. Let cook, pressing down occasionally to make sure entire surface of steak is in contact with skillet, until a deep golden-brown crust forms, about 3 minutes. Transfer to a plate. Without wiping skillet, repeat with second steak.

3 Flip steak and return reserved steak to skillet (browned side up); add 2 tablespoons of the butter, smashed garlic cloves, and thyme to the skillet and cook until butter melts. Carefully tilt skillet so that pan drippings, butter, garlic, and thyme pool at the bottom. Use a large heatproof spoon to baste butter mixture over steaks and continue cooking for 2 to 3 more minutes, until second side has formed a deep golden crust. Use a digital read thermometer to check the temperature of the thickest portion of the ribeye—it should reach 130°F (54°C) for medium-rare. (This will take longer on thicker steaks.) If your steak has not reached 130°F (54°C), place the hot skillet in the preheated oven and continue to cook until a thermometer inserted into the thickest portion of the meat reads 130°F (54°C). Once the steak has come to your desired temperature (even if this means you did not need to continue cooking in the oven), remove steaks from skillet and let rest on a cutting board for 10 minutes before slicing.

4 Meanwhile, remove garlic cloves and thyme from skillet, along with all but 3 tablespoons of the pan drippings. Heat reserved 3 tablespoons pan drippings in skillet over medium-high heat. Add mushrooms to skillet and cook, undisturbed, until golden on one side, about 2 minutes. Continue cooking, stirring occasionally, until golden all over, about 4 more minutes. Add minced garlic to mushrooms and cook until fragrant, about 30 seconds, then add in wine and Worcestershire. Cook 1 to 2 minutes, until reduced by half, then remove from heat. Whisk in remaining 4 tablespoons (55 g) cold butter, 1 tablespoon at a time, off the heat, stirring until butter is melted and incorporated, then season with pepper and remaining ¼ teaspoon salt. If desired, slice steaks against the grain, then top with flaky sea salt. Transfer to two serving plates before dividing sauce evenly between steaks.

Chez Fonfon
dîner
bar
boule
205.939.3221

date-night-in

serving suggestions

In our house, supper prep and clean-up is a joint activity. We have a system. While I cook, I do my chopping on one side of the counter. When I'm done with an ingredient, I move it to the other side of the counter so Luis knows it's ready to be put back. As I keep cooking, he starts on the dishes and sets the table. Then, when we're finished eating, we both work to do what I call "close the diner." We eat supper at home most every night of the week, so this nightly routine often feels mundane. I know y'all can relate.

But, on the occasional weekend night when we have no agenda (a rare feat in our very busy house), we love to throw our own little dinner party for two. I cut flowers from the garden or Luis brings some home, and we use a tablecloth AND chargers. (I know, so fancy!) We pull out our wedding china, because it deserves to be used. We make a bourbon cocktail or open up a good bottle of red, turn on some music, and make the normal dinner routine a little fancier and more fun.

I might try out a new recipe from a cookbook or splurge on prime rib eyes from our local butcher shop (see my favorite way to make them on page 100). We love ending the night with just a little something sweet. If I'm feeling extra generous, I might make a batch of Best-Ever Brownies (page 195), but most times we eat leftovers from my work video shoots or indulge in a pint of the cookies-and-cream-peanut-butter-cup-cookie-dough ice cream we keep in our freezer.

For two people whose most-loved hobby is dressing up to go out to a fancy restaurant (yes, that is considered a hobby), these date nights at home are always such a treat. Something about slowing down, staying home and enjoying little moments together always feels like a boost we didn't know we needed. Even if it does mean doing our own dishes.

Basil
SOUTHERN COOKING

chapter 4

joys and sorrows

In the South, people show up for each other in times of joy and in times of sorrow, as well as the everydays in between. When new neighbors move in or a couple welcomes a baby, we bring food, help out with yard work, and do laundry. The same happens when someone gets sick or a family member passes away. I'm not saying these things don't happen outside the South. They certainly do. But this sense of hospitality is an innate part of Southern culture that seems born of our DNA. There's no need to ask for help because we know it's already on the way.

Right now, my husband, Luis, and I are in the stage of life where our friends are having babies or moving into new houses. With that comes baby showers, wedding showers, and housewarming parties. We keep the meal train circuit hot, and I've gotten my system down to an art. I always make enough dinner to feed the other family and my own, because the last thing I want to do is come home after a social visit and make another meal. If I'm making a dish for a shower, it needs to check all the boxes: able to be made ahead, scaled easily to fit the guest count, and doesn't need to be kept cold or hot for serving. All the recipes in this chapter are my go-tos for times like these. The Green Chile Chicken Enchiladas (page 139) and Christmas Eve Lasagna (page 133) have instructions for making one 9 by 13-inch (23 by 33-cm) or two 8 by 8-inch (20 by 20-cm) dishes, so that you'll have one to take and one to enjoy yourself. There are recipes for Any-Berry Muffins with Cornbread Streusel (page 113) and Orange-Roll Coffee Cake (page 117) that I love to bring to Sunday school breakfast potlucks or new neighbors. The Pimiento Cheese Grits (page 128) and Aunt Patti's Rice Consommé (page 111) are perfect comfort foods for grieving families, and my Easy Granola on page 114 is simple to whip up when you need a last-minute host gift or teacher "happy." Whether you make a recipe from this book or just have time to send a friend an encouraging text, the important thing to remember is that in all of life's joys and sorrows, you just need to show up. The rest doesn't matter.

BASIL

aunt patti's rice consommé

SERVES 6 TO 8
ACTIVE: 20 MINUTES (LESS IF YOU SKIP THE MUSHROOMS)
TOTAL: 1 HOUR, 10 MINUTES (1 HOUR IF YOU SKIP THE MUSHROOMS)

6 tablespoons (85 g) unsalted butter

½ cup (65 g) finely chopped onion

1¼ cups (230 g) extra-long-grain enriched white rice

2 (10.5-ounce / 298-g) cans beef consommé

Optional ingredients:

1 tablespoon extra-virgin olive oil

4 ounces (115 g) sliced baby bella mushrooms

My godmother, Patti Wells, whom I call Aunt Patti, is what Southerners like to call a "hostess with the mostest." Growing up, I had lots of dinners at the Wells' house. Though she's known for her signature Patti Slabs of desserts, I can't help but think of her every time I make rice consommé. She usually serves it alongside roasted pork tenderloin and basil green beans—a meal that I crave often when I need comfort food. As much as I love the rice (it truly is one of my all-time best comfort dishes), I think I love the happy memories it brings to mind even more. I'm lucky enough to have so many strong women in my life who've inspired my love of hosting. She gave me a love for blue and white, classic Southern style, Armetale dinnerware, big slices of cake, and recipes (like this rice) that make everyone feel at home.

1. Preheat oven to 375°F (190°C). In a medium nonstick skillet, melt butter over medium heat. When butter is melted, pour 4 tablespoons of the butter into a 2-quart (2-L) baking dish, leaving the remaining 2 tablespoons butter in the skillet.
2. Add onion to skillet and cook over medium heat, stirring often, until onions start to soften, about 4 minutes. Add rice to onion in skillet and cook, stirring often, until onions are translucent and soft and rice begins to brown and smell nutty, 4 to 5 minutes.
3. Add rice and onion to butter in baking dish with beef consommé; stir to combine.
4. Cover baking dish tightly with aluminum foil and bake in preheated oven until rice is tender and no liquid remains in the dish, 45 to 50 minutes. Serve immediately, or see cook's note about optional mushrooms.

ivy's take! This rice dish is known by many as "stick of butter rice" or rice consommé. Many recipes call for adding canned mushrooms, but I like to go the extra step to cook my own. Freshly sauteed mushrooms are SO much better than canned and well worth it—BUT mushrooms aren't for everybody, so it is totally acceptable to skip this step if you want! If you do want to add in mushrooms: While rice cooks, heat 1 tablespoon olive oil in a medium skillet over high heat. Add 4 ounces (115 g) sliced mushrooms and cook, stirring occasionally, until mushrooms are golden brown and all liquid has evaporated from the skillet, about 7 minutes. Add mushrooms to the top of the rice when it comes out of the oven to serve.

any-berry muffins with cornmeal streusel

MAKES 1 DOZEN
ACTIVE: 15 MINUTES
TOTAL: 50 MINUTES

1½ teaspoons baking powder

½ teaspoon salt

1⅔ cups (205 g) all-purpose flour, divided

⅓ cup (45 g) plus 2 tablespoons plain yellow cornmeal, divided

1 cup (200 g) granulated sugar, divided

½ cup (120 ml) melted unsalted butter, divided

½ cup (120 ml) whole buttermilk

1 large egg

1 large egg yolk

1½ teaspoons vanilla extract

1⅓ cups (185 g) fresh berries, such as strawberries, blueberries, raspberries, or blackberries

This is one of the very first recipes I had published in *Southern Living* magazine. I developed it long before I ever started making videos or had a recipe column in print. I was so proud of it then, and I never in a million years thought it would end up in a cookbook. Years later, these are still my go-to muffins, and every time I bake a batch, I think of how far I've come.

1. Preheat oven to 425°F (220°C). Line a 12-cup muffin pan with paper cupcake liners. In a medium bowl, whisk together baking powder, salt, 1⅓ cups (165 g) of the flour, and ⅓ cup (45 g) of the cornmeal; set aside.

2. In a separate bowl, stir together ¼ cup (50 g) of the sugar, 3 tablespoons of the melted butter, and remaining ⅓ cup (40 g) flour and 2 tablespoons cornmeal until crumbly; reserve for streusel topping.

3. In a medium bowl, whisk together buttermilk, egg and yolk, vanilla, and remaining ¾ cup (150 g) sugar until well-combined. Make a well in center of flour mixture. Slowly pour buttermilk mixture into flour mixture, stirring with a spatula until just combined. (It will be lumpy.) Fold in berries and remaining 5 tablespoons (75 ml) melted butter.

4. Scoop batter into prepared pan until each cup is three-fourths full (about 3 tablespoons each). Top each with about 1 tablespoon reserved streusel topping. Bake in preheated oven until a wooden pick inserted in center of each muffin comes out clean, about 18 minutes. Remove from oven; cool in pan for 5 minutes. Cool muffins on a wire rack, about 10 minutes.

easy granola

MAKES ABOUT 4 CUPS (400 G)
ACTIVE: 10 MINUTES
TOTAL: 1 HOUR, 35 MINUTES

3 cups (270 g) old-fashioned rolled oats

⅓ cup (75 ml) extra-virgin olive oil

⅓ cup (75 ml) pure maple syrup

⅓ cup (75 g) packed light brown sugar

1 teaspoon kosher salt

½ teaspoon ground cinnamon

¼ teaspoon ground cardamom

1 large egg white, beaten

If you've never made your own granola, you'll be shocked at how easy (and so much better than store-bought) it is. This simple recipe can be customized with any kind of stir-ins, like dried fruit, toasted nuts and seeds, or chocolate chips—just be sure to add them in once it's cool. I love bringing a batch of granola along with a meal for new parents, so that supper AND breakfast are two less things on their to-do list.

1. Preheat oven to 300°F (150°C). In a large bowl, toss together oats, oil, syrup, brown sugar, salt, cinnamon, cardamom, and egg white until oats are well coated; spread in a single layer on a large parchment paper–lined baking sheet.

2. Bake in preheated oven until golden brown, crisp, and mostly dry, about 45 minutes, stirring every 15 minutes. (Granola will continue to crisp as it cools.) Let cool completely on baking sheet on a wire rack, 30 to 45 minutes. Store in an airtight container up to 10 days.

orange-roll coffee cake

SERVES 12
ACTIVE: 25 MINUTES
TOTAL: 3 HOURS, 30 MINUTES

3¾ cups (14⅛ ounces / 404 g) bleached cake flour, such as Swans Down, divided, plus more for tube pan

1½ cups (330 g) packed light brown sugar, divided

2⅛ teaspoons grated orange zest, plus 1 to 2 tablespoons fresh juice (from 2 navel oranges), divided

1½ teaspoons kosher salt, divided

¼ teaspoon ground nutmeg, divided

1 cup (8 ounces / 227 g) unsalted butter, softened and divided, plus more for tube pan

1 cup (200 g) granulated sugar

10 ounces (280 g) cream cheese, softened and divided

4 large eggs

1 teaspoon vanilla extract

2 teaspoons baking powder

¼ teaspoon baking soda

¼ cup (30 g) powdered sugar

I'd never eaten, let alone heard of, an orange roll until I moved to Birmingham. Here, the sweet rolls are as commonplace as coffee cakes are where I'm from in Georgia. They are sweet enough to be served as a dessert, but not so sweet that they can't pass as breakfast. My orange-roll coffee cake combines the two like a hug from my past and a celebration of my present. I love how certain foods ground us and make us feel right at home, no matter where we are. Whether you make this for breakfast, dessert, or for a new neighbor or the church picnic, I hope it makes everyone who tastes it feel right at home.

1. In a large bowl, stir together 1¼ cups (165 g) of the flour, 1 cup (220 g) of the brown sugar, 1 teaspoon of the zest, 1 teaspoon of the salt, and ⅛ teaspoon of the nutmeg. Place ¼ cup (55 g) of the butter in a microwavable dish. Microwave on high until melted, about 30 seconds. Add to flour mixture and stir until mixture starts to clump together in small crumbles. Cover and chill until ready to use.

2. Preheat oven to 350°F (175°C). Lightly grease a 10-inch (25-cm) tube pan with butter and dust with flour; set aside. In a medium bowl, stir together granulated sugar, 1 teaspoon of the zest, and remaining ½ cup (110 g) brown sugar, rubbing zest and sugars between your fingers to release oils from zest and to fully incorporate into sugar; set aside. In the bowl of a stand mixer fitted with a paddle attachment, beat 8 ounces (225 g) of the cream cheese and remaining ¾ cup (170 g) butter on medium speed until smooth, about 1 minute. Add sugar mixture to cream cheese mixture, and beat on medium speed until light and fluffy, about 4 minutes. Add eggs, 1 at a time, beating well after each addition, stopping to scrape down sides of bowl as needed. Stir in vanilla until combined.

3. In a medium bowl, stir together baking powder, baking soda, and remaining 2½ cups (325 g) flour, ½ teaspoon salt, and ⅛ teaspoon nutmeg. Gradually add flour mixture to cream cheese mixture, beating on low speed until just combined, about 2 minutes. Spoon half of batter (about 2 cups / 480 ml) into prepared tube pan, spreading

continued

into an even layer. Top evenly with half of reserved crumble mixture (about 1¼ cups / 255 g). Repeat layers once using remaining batter and crumble mixture.

4 Bake in preheated oven until a wooden pick inserted in center comes out clean, 50 to 55 minutes, tenting with aluminum foil after 35 minutes, if needed, to prevent excessive browning. Cool cake in tube pan on a wire rack for 15 minutes. Invert cake onto a plate, then invert again onto wire rack so crumble mixture is on top. Let cool completely, about 2 hours.

5 In the bowl of an electric mixer, beat powdered sugar, 1 tablespoon of the orange juice, and remaining ⅛ teaspoon orange zest and 2 ounces (55 g) cream cheese with an electric mixer on medium speed until smooth, about 1 minute. Add up to remaining 1 tablespoon orange juice, 1 teaspoon at a time, until desired consistency is reached. Drizzle glaze over cooled cake; serve with any additional glaze.

---

if this isn't southern . . . When making this recipe, I turn to my heirloom old-school tube pan, but a Bundt pan will also do the trick. One of my favorites is the Nordic Ware Anniversary Bundt, which has a pretty fluted shape and handles for easy unmolding.

pimiento cheese–sausage pinwheels

SERVES 12
ACTIVE: 15 MINUTES
TOTAL: 1 HOUR, 40 MINUTES

1 pound (455 g) refrigerated pizza dough

12 ounces (340 g) bulk hot pork sausage

1 cup (4 ounces / 115 g) shredded sharp Cheddar cheese, plus more for sprinkling

½ cup (4 ounces / 115 g) cream cheese, softened

1 (7-ounce / 198-g) jar diced pimientos, drained

1 tablespoon grated sweet onion (from 1 small onion)

1 teaspoon garlic powder

All-purpose flour

Cooking spray

Growing up, Christmas breakfast at my nana and papa's house was an elaborate Southern affair. The special Franciscan Ivy china and coordinating green glassware was pulled from the cabinet a week before, cleaned, and set on dining tables draped with Christmas tablecloths. Christmas morning, while the grandchildren were up early opening presents at our own houses, Nana was already busy at the stove. The menu was extensive: biscuits, yeast rolls, link and patty sausages, bacon, fried cube steak with gravy, rice, grits, and even eggs cooked to order. If you noticed a lot of overlap (namely meats, breads, and starches), it was intentional. Since no one agreed on their favorites, Nana just made it all.

While Nana has always been a fine cook, she is known for some signature dishes: the aforementioned Christmas breakfast, teacakes, and pimiento cheese. She always had a Country Crock tub full of that cheesy delicacy in her fridge. I was known to sneak a bite here and there with a roll and piece of bacon and wondered why pimiento cheese never made its way onto the Christmas breakfast menu. The Christmas breakfast torch has been passed on to my mama and me nowadays, and while we mostly stick to Nana's menu (she'd have a fit if we didn't), I put my own spin on her classics, whether it's a new biscuit recipe, a special gravy, or a delicious mashup like these pimiento cheese–sausage pinwheels. They're my way of sneaking Nana's famous pimiento cheese onto our Christmas plates. They also are a terrific addition to a game-day spread—something Papa considers as important as any Christmas menu. Whether accompanied by grits and eggs or chicken wings and pickled okra, one bite of these savory rolls brings up sweet memories of Nana and my South Georgia home.

1 Let pizza dough stand, covered, at room temperature, until no longer cold to the touch, about 30 minutes. Meanwhile, in a large bowl, place sausage, Cheddar, cream cheese, pimientos, onion, and garlic powder. Using your hands or a rubber spatula, mix ingredients together until well-combined. Cover and refrigerate until ready to use.

continued

2 Preheat oven to 375°F (190°C). Roll dough out on a lightly floured work surface and stretch into a 16 by 12-inch (40.5 x 30.5-cm) rectangle. Using an offset spatula or your hands, spread sausage mixture evenly over dough rectangle, leaving a ½-inch (12-mm) border on each long edge of dough and spreading fully out to shorter edges of dough. Starting with one long edge, roll dough up, jelly-roll style, to create one long log. Using a serrated knife, cut log crosswise evenly into 12 (about 1¼-inch-wide / 3-cm) slices.

3 Lightly grease a 7 by 11-inch (17 by 28-cm) glass or ceramic baking dish with cooking spray. Arrange sausage rolls in prepared baking dish in 4 rows of 3 rolls each. Sprinkle tops of rolls with desired amount of Cheddar; cover dish with aluminum foil.

4 Bake in preheated oven for 20 minutes. Remove foil from baking dish and continue baking until rolls are golden brown and a thermometer inserted into thickest portion of sausage registers 165°F (74°C), 20 to 25 minutes. Remove from oven, and let stand 10 minutes. Serve. Pinwheels may be stored, covered, in refrigerator, up to 3 days.

When people first find out that I cook for a living, most immediately respond, "What's your favorite thing to make?" The honest answer is, well, pretty much everything. I prefer savory cooking over baking, but when prompted with this question, my mind is flooded with the memory of a cake from my childhood.

I was over at my friend Hannah's house to play when her mama asked if I wanted to help gather eggs at the neighbor's house, and I jumped at the chance. We got six eggs—just enough for a pound cake, she said. To my picky twelve-year-old palate, pound cake didn't sound too exciting, but the prospect of being in the kitchen was impossible to refuse.

Mrs. Heather pulled out her big KitchenAid mixer and started creaming together the butter, cream cheese, and sugar while I cracked the eggs. She let me add them in, one at a time, and I couldn't hide my excitement as I watched the swirls of yellow yolk blend into the smooth, pale batter. We put the tube pan into a cold oven, a phenomenon that flabbergasted this novice baker. The smell of the rising caramelized crust filled the house, making those two hours of anticipation the longest wait of my life. I barely got to have a slice before it was time for me to go home, but one bite of the warm, buttery cake was enough to change my life forever.

I had never liked a pound cake before that day. Nor had I gathered eggs or used a fancy stand mixer—two more firsts that further solidified the experience as one of the most memorable days of my life. I came home begging my parents for a KitchenAid mixer of my own, fully convinced I couldn't make the world's best pound cake without it. They finally gave in when I turned thirteen. I remember hoisting the shiny baby pink mixer onto the counter for the first time and running to the fridge to see if we had any cream cheese. The pink mixer's maiden voyage was Mrs. Heather's pound cake.

In the years since, my mixer has moved with me seven times and made more pound cakes than I can remember. I've made a few tweaks to the recipe over the years, like the addition of bourbon and almond extract. Even so, no matter that I graduated top in my class from culinary school or spent half a dozen years in the *Southern Living* Test Kitchen, to this day, the most-requested recipe of my friends and family is the one my prized pink mixer knows by heart.

ivy's favorite pound cake

SERVES 18
ACTIVE: 20 MINUTES
TOTAL: 4 HOURS, 20 MINUTES, INCLUDING 2 HOURS COOLING

Cooking spray

3 cups (11¼ ounces / 317 g) bleached cake flour, such as Swans Down, plus more for tube pan

3 cups (600 g) granulated sugar

1½ cups (12 ounces / 340 g) salted butter, softened

1 (8-ounce / 226-g) package cream cheese, softened

6 large eggs

2 teaspoons bourbon

2 teaspoons fresh lemon juice (from 1 lemon)

1 teaspoon vanilla extract

½ teaspoon almond extract

¼ teaspoon kosher salt

The secret to the best pound cake is a cold oven. I know the cardinal rule of every baking recipe is "always be sure to preheat the oven," but this is one exception. By starting the cake in a cold oven, you end with a thick, golden, caramelized crust reminiscent of a crunchy meringue. I've also never met a pound cake lighter and fluffier than one that started in a cold oven. Baking it low and slow gives the leavening more time to work before the cake sets, making it taller and fluffier. Plus, the thick crust locks in moisture, helping the cake stay moist longer. So many benefits! You'd be silly not to try it.

1. Coat a light-colored 18-cup / 4.3-L (10-inch / 25-cm) tube pan with cooking spray and lightly dust with flour. Set aside. Do not preheat oven. In a stand mixer fitted with a paddle attachment, beat sugar and butter on medium-high speed until mixture is light and fluffy, about 3 minutes. Beat in cream cheese until smooth, about 30 seconds. Add eggs, 1 at a time, beating on low speed until just combined.

2. Add flour, 1 cup (125 g) at a time, beating on low speed until blended after each addition, about 1 minute total, and stopping to scrape down sides of bowl as needed. Beat in bourbon, lemon juice, vanilla, almond extract, and salt until smooth. Transfer batter to prepared pan and smooth top.

3. Place on rack in lower third of a cold, un-preheated oven. Turn oven on to 300°F (150°C) and bake until a wooden pick inserted into center of the cake comes out clean, 1 hour, 50 minutes to 2 hours. Let cool in pan 30 minutes. Run an offset spatula around edges of cake to loosen; remove from pan and let cool completely on a wire rack, about 1 hour, 30 minutes.

marinated shrimp pasta salad

SERVES 6
ACTIVE: 30 MINUTES
TOTAL: 45 MINUTES

12 cups (2.8 L) water, plus more as needed

3 tablespoons plus ¼ teaspoon kosher salt, divided

12 ounces (340 g) uncooked orecchiette pasta

3 tablespoons, plus ¾ teaspoon lower-sodium Old Bay seasoning, divided

1 pound (455 g) medium raw shrimp, peeled and deveined

¼ cup (60 ml) fresh lemon juice (from 2 lemons)

1 tablespoon coarse-grained Dijon mustard

1 tablespoon honey

1 cup (240 ml) extra-virgin olive oil

1 teaspoon minced garlic (from 2 medium garlic cloves)

½ teaspoon crushed red pepper

¼ teaspoon freshly ground black pepper

6 multicolored sweet mini peppers, cut into thin rings (2 cups / 6 ounces / 170 g)

2 medium shallots, thinly sliced (½ cup / 1½ ounces / 40 g)

½ cup (50 g) thinly sliced celery (from 2 stalks)

½ cup (25 g) roughly chopped fresh dill

¼ cup (13 g) roughly chopped fresh flat-leaf parsley

There's just something about pickled shrimp that makes me giddy. It really is a beautiful dish, with perfectly curled pink shrimp nestled among vibrant crisp vegetables and herbs, all tossed together in a light vinaigrette studded with whole pickling spices. Unlike some recipes that haven't stood the test of time, this old-school Southern delicacy, known to many as Sea Island shrimp, still feels like a modern luxury. Every time I eat it, I say to myself, "I should make this more often!" This twist on pasta salad is now a staple in my house come outdoor entertaining weather. It's packed full of fresh herbs, peak-of-season veggies, and all my favorite pickled shrimp flavors. I make it ahead, because it gets better the longer it sits, and I take it outside to serve in my outdoor kitchen, where you can find me all spring.

1 Fill a large bowl with ice and water; set aside. In a large stockpot, bring 12 cups (2.8 L) water and 3 tablespoons of the salt to a boil over medium-high heat. Add pasta and cook, stirring occasionally, until al dente, about 12 minutes. Using a spider or slotted spoon, transfer pasta from boiling water to a baking sheet lined with paper towels; let cool completely, about 10 minutes. Do not remove boiling water from heat.

2 Add 3 tablespoons of the Old Bay seasoning to boiling water and boil for 2 minutes. Add shrimp and cook, undisturbed, until just pink and just cooked through, about 2 minutes; drain. Transfer shrimp immediately to ice water; let cool completely, about 7 minutes.

3 Meanwhile, in a medium bowl, whisk together lemon juice, mustard, and honey. Gradually whisk in oil until thickened and combined. Whisk in garlic, crushed red pepper, black pepper, and remaining ¼ teaspoon salt and ¾ teaspoon Old Bay seasoning until combined.

4 Place pasta, shrimp, mini peppers, shallots, celery, dill, and parsley in a large bowl; add vinaigrette and toss until well coated. Serve immediately, or cover and store in refrigerator up to 24 hours.

tip: Switch up the veggies as the seasons change!

pimiento cheese grits

SERVES 8
ACTIVE: 15 MINUTES
TOTAL: 15 MINUTES

2 cups (480 ml) chicken (or vegetable) broth

2 cups (480 ml) whole milk

½ teaspoon kosher salt

1 cup (170 g) enriched grits (yellow or white)

1 cup (248 g) My Favorite Pimiento Cheese (page 154), or any pimiento cheese

Thinly sliced green onions, for garnish (optional)

This recipe calls for enriched grits, which take significantly less time to cook than stone-ground ones. If you have the time, stone-ground grits are well worth it. Follow the manufacturer's instructions for the ratio of grits to liquid, using half whole milk and half chicken (or vegetable) broth for the best flavor. In the mornings, I rarely have the patience to cook stone-ground grits, which is why I've written a recipe for enriched ones. But if you're more patient than me, by all means go for it. If you're planning on taking these anywhere, adding in a half cup more milk than I call for will ensure the grits don't become too stiff before they make it to their final destination.

In a medium saucepan, bring chicken broth, milk, and salt to a boil over medium-high heat. Whisk in grits, reduce heat to medium-low, and cook, stirring very often, until thickened and grits are tender, 5 to 6 minutes. Remove from heat and whisk in pimiento cheese until melted. Serve immediately and garnish with green onions, if desired.

behind the scenes I first came up with the idea for pimiento cheese grits when I was planning the menu for the *Southern Living* UNwineD event in Panama City Beach, Florida. I worked with the amazing team at Townsend Catering, who helped bring my recipes and menu to life. The pimiento cheese grits we served at the event were such a hit, and I was right smack in the middle of cookbook planning, so I knew they had to come to life in the book. Now, it's the only way I make my cheese grits.

I've always been fascinated by what other people eat the night before Christmas. In the company of standing rib roasts, baked hams, tamales, or cornbread dressing, my family's traditional Christmas Eve lasagna seemed a little ordinary. Don't get me wrong, our table was adorned beautifully with full settings of Lenox Holiday china, the "good silver," my great-grandmother's hand-embroidered linens, crystal goblets, and an over-the-top centerpiece. And, it wasn't like we made lasagna very often. In fact, we only ever ate it twice a year—once on Christmas Eve, as per our custom, and on a random night a few months later, because we always had enough fixings left over for another casserole dish to be enjoyed when Mama needed to pull something out of the freezer to feed us. Like all the best family recipes, this lasagna was passed down to my dad from his Mémère, my great-grandmother, in the way so many great family recipes are shared—by word of mouth. In her very thick French-Canadian-in-Connecticut accent, she would say the layers out loud as she assembled them. Eager to learn the secret to her famous dish, my dad remembers listening to her chant, "meat sauce, cottage cheese, cheese, noodles." For my entire childhood, this is how we made ours. Until one year, my mama pointed out that most lasgna recipes use ricotta, not cottage cheese.

Though we loved it as is, we called my great-aunt (Mémère's daughter) to confirm. Either due to the strong accent or my dad's foggy memory, somewhere along the line ricotta was misconstrued as "cottage." We were told that the lasagna we'd been making for years was, indeed, incorrect. Disheartened that his fond memory of his grandmother's lasagna layer chant was wrong, my dad agreed to try making it with ricotta that year. The result was dismal in comparison to our usual cottage cheese version. We've since always assembled our night-before-Christmas lasagna the way we like it, replacing the family's tradition with what turned out to be a nontraditional approach.

As I've gotten older, I've realized my family's Christmas Eve meal is anything but ordinary. It might not have the grandeur of a standing rib roast, and it might not even be considered real lasagna to some. But for me, it represents that special way new generations create their own Christmas Eve traditions (with or without cottage cheese). I believe Mémère would be proud of that.

ivy's take! This lasagna can also be made in two 8 by 8-inch (20 by 20-cm) baking dishes. Cut cooked noodles in half to fit, then follow recipe instructions as directed, dividing ingredients evenly between both dishes. Bake, covered, for 30 minutes. Uncover, then continue baking another 20 to 25 minutes, until edges are bubbly and cheese is browned in some spots.

christmas eve lasagna

SERVES 8
ACTIVE: 40 MINUTES
TOTAL: 1 HOUR, 35 MINUTES

2 teaspoons extra-virgin olive oil

¾ pound (340 g) ground beef round (85/15)

½ pound (225 g) hot Italian pork sausage

½ cup (65 g) finely chopped sweet onion (from 1 small onion)

½ cup (75 g) finely chopped red bell pepper (from 1 small pepper)

2 tablespoons minced garlic (from 6 medium cloves)

¼ cup (60 g) tomato paste (from one 6-ounce / 170-g can)

1 (28-ounce / 794-g) can crushed tomatoes

2 teaspoons Italian seasoning

1¾ teaspoons kosher salt

¾ teaspoon granulated sugar

½ teaspoon freshly ground black pepper

½ teaspoon Worcestershire sauce

9 lasagna noodles (from one 16-ounce / 453-g package)

18 (¾-ounce / 21-g) slices low-moisture part-skim mozzarella, or 6 cups (660 g) shredded

1 (16-ounce / 453-g) container whole milk small curd cottage cheese

½ cup (2 ounces / 55 g) freshly grated Parmesan cheese

Cooking spray

If you find the whole idea of cottage cheese in your lasagna a little too nontraditional, ricotta will work in its place. But do me a favor and try it just once with cottage cheese. You might be surprised by how much you like it!

1 In a 5-quart (4.7-L) Dutch oven, heat oil over medium-high heat. Add ground beef and sausage and cook, stirring to crumble, until meat starts to brown but some pink still remains, 2 to 3 minutes. Add onion and bell pepper to meat and cook, continuing to stir and crumble meat, until vegetables are soft and meat is fully browned, about 4 more minutes. Add garlic and cook, stirring constantly, until fragrant, about 1 minute.

2 Add tomato paste to meat mixture and stir to coat meat well in tomato paste. Cook, stirring often, until tomato paste starts to caramelize, about 3 minutes. Stir in crushed tomatoes, Italian seasoning, salt, sugar, and black pepper. Bring to a boil, then reduce heat to medium-low and simmer 20 minutes, or until mixture is reduced slightly. Stir in Worcestershire and remove from heat. Proceed with assembling lasagna immediately, or let cool 30 minutes at room temperature before transferring meat sauce to an airtight container and refrigerating for up to 3 days before using. Alternatively, freeze for up to 4 months. Thaw completely before using.

3 When ready to assemble lasagna, preheat oven to 350°F (175°C), and cook noodles according to package directions in heavily salted water. Drain noodles well.

4 Spoon ½ cup (120 ml) meat sauce in an even layer in the bottom of a 9 by 13-inch (23 x 33-cm) baking dish. Layer 3 noodles on top of the meat sauce, then top with about 1½ cups meat sauce. Spread one-third of the cottage cheese (about ½ cup / 151 g) evenly over the meat sauce, then top with 6 slices mozzarella. Repeat layers two more times, topping the last layer of mozzarella evenly with Parmesan. Cover dish with aluminum foil lightly greased with cooking spray. Bake in preheated oven until bubbling around the edges, about 30 minutes, then uncover and continue baking another 25 to 30 minutes, until edges are bubbly and cheese is browned in some spots. Remove from oven and let sit 10 minutes before serving.

STANLEY
SINCE 1913
Well
Soon
Fluted
Tapers
ATHENS WINE COMPANY

spread the love

serving suggestions

The thing about most of life's joys and sorrows is that you really never know exactly when they're going to come, so it's good to be prepared with some go-to ideas for anything life throws your way. I like to keep a few gifting supplies, like ribbons, cellophane bags, and cute stationery on hand for when I need to throw together a little "happy."

One of the cardinal rules of being a Southerner is to never show up empty-handed—even if the host tells you not to bring a thing. For cases like these, I love to have candles, bottles of wine or olive oil, cheese straws, linen cocktail napkins, or a batch of my Easy Granola (page 114) at the ready to tie up with a ribbon and be on my way. It's little things like these that really go a long way to make anyone feel appreciated.

basil
agave
gin or bourbon
SOUTHERN
COOKING
Congratulations!

green chile chicken enchiladas

SERVES 8
ACTIVE: 30 MINUTES
TOTAL: 1 HOUR

Cooking spray

2 tablespoons bacon grease or olive oil

1½ cups (165 g) chopped sweet onion (from 1 medium onion)

1 tablespoon minced garlic (from 3 cloves)

1 cup (240 ml) low-sodium chicken broth

1 (7-ounce / 198-g) can chopped green chiles, drained

½ cup (120 ml) whole milk

2 teaspoons Better Than Bouillon roasted chicken paste

2 cups (480 ml) Homemade Cream of Chicken Soup (page 32), or two 10.5-ounce (298-g) cans cream of chicken soup

3 cups (594 g) cooked, shredded, or chopped chicken (from 1 rotisserie chicken)

1½ teaspoons kosher salt

10 corn tortillas, torn into 4 pieces each

4 cups (456 g) shredded Mexican blend cheese

My friend Paige's Aunt Alma makes the best green chile chicken enchiladas in the world. She lives in Hatch, New Mexico, in the heart of the valley where the famous Hatch green chiles are grown. I'm lucky enough to get to spend a few days at her home each fall, putting up chiles to make red enchilada sauce. Over the years, she's taught me a lot about New Mexico cuisine. To properly make pinto beans, you need a dedicated bean pot and salt pork. The secret to the best burritos is SPAM, and if you want good enchiladas you need fresh tortillas fried in good, old-fashioned lard. My recipe for green chile chicken enchiladas isn't exactly like Alma's—I take a few shortcuts. But, for skipping a few steps, it's pretty close. And for me, it gets the job done until I can make it back to Hatch for the best in the world.

1. Preheat oven to 350°F (175°C). Spray one 9 by 13-inch (23 by 33-cm) or two 8 by 8-inch (20 by 20-cm) baking dishes with cooking spray. In a large skillet, heat bacon grease (or olive oil) over medium heat. Add onion to skillet and cook, stirring occasionally, until soft, 7 to 8 minutes. Add garlic to skillet and cook, stirring occasionally, until fragrant, about 1 minute.

2. Stir in chicken broth, green chiles, milk, and bouillon paste. Cook, stirring constantly, until bouillon is incorporated, about 1 minute. Stir in cream of chicken soup and bring to a simmer over medium heat. Simmer until mixture thickens and reduces slightly, about 7 minutes. Stir in chicken and salt, then remove from heat.

3. Assemble and bake the enchiladas: If using a 9 by 13-inch (23 by 33-cm) dish, spread 2 cups of the chicken mixture in an even layer in bottom of baking dish. Top with half of the torn tortilla pieces, then 1⅓ cups (152 g) of the cheese. Repeat with another 2 cups (390 g) chicken mixture, remaining half of the tortillas, and another 1⅓ cups (152 g) of the cheese. Spoon the remaining chicken mixture in an even layer in dish and top with remaining 1⅓ cups (152 g) cheese. Bake in preheated oven until cheese is golden brown and edges are bubbly, 30 to 35 minutes.

note: If using two 8 by 8-inch (20 by 20-cm) dishes, follow the recipe as described above, dividing ingredients evenly between both dishes. Bake in preheated oven until cheese is golden brown and edges are bubbly, 20 to 25 minutes. (Alternatively, you can bake one dish and freeze the other.)

aunt brenda's sour cream banana pudding

SERVES 12
ACTIVE: 25 MINUTES
TOTAL: 4 HOURS, 25 MINUTES, INCLUDING 4 HOURS CHILLING

2 cups (480 ml) cold whole milk

1 (5.1-ounce / 144-g) package vanilla instant pudding and pie filling

3 cups (720 ml) heavy whipping cream

½ cup (2 ounces / 55 g) powdered sugar

1 teaspoon vanilla extract

1 (8-ounce / 227-g) container sour cream

1 (14-ounce / 397-g) can sweetened condensed milk

8 cups vanilla wafers (from two 11-ounce / 311-g packages)

2½ pounds (1.2 kg) spotted ripe bananas, cut into ⅛-inch-thick slices

Growing up, I was a strict rule follower. But, come my birthday in mid-April, I could be counted on to do one thing that was against the rules. Before supper, I would sneak into the refrigerator to eat a heaping scoop of my Aunt Brenda's famous banana pudding. Because it was my birthday, my parents pretended not to notice the dent in the pudding come dessert time. As her gift to me, my aunt always made a big bowl of her banana pudding.

Her recipe is the standard to which I hold every other banana pudding. Her secret? Sour cream! No banana pudding I've tried can hold a birthday candle to Aunt Brenda's recipe. The added tang and creaminess balances what often can be a too-sweet-to-finish dessert. Aunt Brenda's banana pudding is most definitely one of the reasons I prefer gifts that can be experienced. Memories of sneaking a bite every year on my birthday, getting to eat leftover pudding for breakfast the next day, and eventually receiving her recipe as a gift so that I could carry on the tradition of making her famous pudding for all our gatherings, is far superior to anything she could've wrapped up in a bow.

1 In a large bowl or 8-cup (2 L) measuring cup, whisk together milk and pudding and pie filling until smooth. Let stand until very thick, 5 to 7 minutes. Meanwhile, in a separate large bowl, beat heavy whipping cream with an electric mixer on high speed until soft peaks form, 1 to 2 minutes. Gradually add powdered sugar and beat until stiff peaks form, 30 seconds to 1 minute. Stir in vanilla. Reserve 1½ cups (360 ml) of the whipped cream in a small bowl; set aside.

2 Whisk sour cream and sweetened condensed milk into thickened pudding until smooth. Fold in remaining whipped cream until smooth and light.

3 In a 3-quart (2.8 L) trifle dish or straight-sided serving bowl, arrange about 12 vanilla wafers in a single layer in bottom of dish. Top vanilla wafers with about ¾ cup (113 g) of the banana slices; top banana slices with about 1 cup (240 ml) of the pudding mixture.

4 Stand about 12 vanilla wafers along sides of dish on top of pudding mixture layer to create second layer. Arrange about 18 vanilla wafers on top of pudding mixture in a single layer. Top vanilla wafers with about ¾ cup (113 g) of the banana slices and about 1 cup (240 ml) of the pudding mixture.

5 Arrange about 12 vanilla wafers in a single layer over the pudding mixture; stand about 20 banana slices along sides of dish on top of vanilla wafer layer. Arrange about 20 banana slices on top of vanilla wafers in center of dish to make a single layer; top evenly with about 1 cup (240 ml) of the pudding mixture. Repeat layering process two times with remaining vanilla wafers (reserving 4 or 5 for garnishing later on), banana slices, and pudding mixture, ending with a layer of pudding mixture.

6 Spoon reserved 1½ cups (360 ml) whipped cream onto center of pudding mixture. With back of a large spoon or offset spatula, slowly spread whipped cream to edges, leaving most of whipped cream in a mound in center of pudding. Lightly crush remaining 4 to 5 vanilla wafers to create large crumbs, and sprinkle over center of whipped cream. Store, covered, in refrigerator at least 4 hours or up to 24 hours.

chapter 5

lawn parties

When I think of lawn parties, the first thing that pops into my mind is the annual Back-to-School Blues Barbecue my parents threw at the end of every summer. My mama was a teacher, so it was her last hurrah before the start of a new school year. She and Daddy love any excuse to have people over, and Back-to-School Blues was just as much a party for them as it was for all the neighborhood kids and their families. Like any good nineties backyard party, Hootie & the Blowfish played while the adults toasted the start of school and the kids enjoyed water games. (I was especially a fan of the Crazy Daisy sprinkler.) Barbecue was always on the menu, along with a plethora of Southern sides. The food at my parents' parties never disappoints, but it is their ability to make everyone feel welcome that really made those annual events so memorable. They set a high bar with those Back-to-School Blues parties, one I strive to meet each time I host a gathering of my own nowadays. Theirs are some pretty big shoes to fill, but I love a good challenge.

There is something about taking a party to the yard that lends a more laid-back vibe to the occasion, whether it's a seated dinner party or a casual cookout. Because I am my mother's daughter, I simply cannot throw a party, indoors or out, without making it a big to-do. When we do something, we do it RIGHT or not at all. So, there will be a theme, there must be decorations, and Lord willing and the creek don't rise, every guest will leave feeling like they were a part of something special. I learned all my best hosting tips from my mama. Together, we planned the most epic outdoor party—my garden party wedding reception. There's plenty more about that beginning on page 43.

The recipes featured in this chapter are dishes I love to serve when the occasion calls for a good old-fashioned lawn party. From tailgates to the Masters, some dishes are tailored to fit those featured party themes. The other recipes you'll find on the pages that follow are just so delicious that no lawn parties chapter in my book would be complete if I didn't share them with you. I hope you'll weave them into whatever lawn party theme you might dream up.

The Whipped Goat Cheese with Bacon Jam (page 177) and Pumpkin Whoopie Pies (page 196) are great examples. But, like my memories of those Back-to-School Blues Barbecues, the menu doesn't make a good party a great one. (Though delicious food does help!) My mama taught me that hospitality is a gift, and that if you love something you should share it. Our family loves throwing parties because they're an excuse to share what we love most with the people we love most. Parties can be a lot of work, but if you plan well and prep ahead, following my mama's number one rule of party-throwing—having fun—will be easy! It is *your* party, after all.

dilly potato salad
(page 148)

party potato salad (page 149)

dilly potato salad

SERVES 6
ACTIVE: 20 MINUTES
TOTAL: 1 HOUR

2¼ pounds (1 kg) Yukon Gold potatoes, cut into 1-inch (2.5-cm) chunks

2 tablespoons extra-virgin olive oil

2 teaspoons kosher salt, divided

⅓ cup (75 ml) sour cream

2 tablespoons mayonnaise

¼ teaspoon garlic powder

¼ teaspoon onion powder

½ teaspoon freshly ground black pepper

½ cup (30 g) thinly sliced green onions (from 4 green onions)

¼ cup (60 ml) finely chopped garlicky sweet pickles, such as Wickles

¼ cup (13 g) chopped fresh dill, plus more for garnish

When I came up with the initial list of recipes for this book, I knew my Party Potato Salad (page 149) had to be included. But toward the end of my recipe development, when I made the recipe for Roasted Smashed Potatoes (page 94), I threw together a potato salad with the leftovers that blew both Luis and me away. The result was basically this dilly potato salad. From experience, I can say it works great with leftover roasted potatoes, but since leftover potatoes are pretty hard to come by, in my house at least, the recipe gives instructions for roasting your own.

1 Preheat oven to 450°F (230°C). Line a rimmed baking sheet with parchment paper. In a large bowl, combine potatoes with oil and 1 teaspoon of the salt; toss well to coat. Set bowl aside to use later, then spread potatoes in an even layer on prepared baking sheet and bake in preheated oven for 30 minutes, or until potatoes are golden and crisp on the edges and fork tender. Remove potatoes from oven and let stand at room temperature for 10 minutes.

2 Meanwhile, in a small bowl, stir together sour cream, mayonnaise, garlic powder, onion powder, pepper, and remaining 1 teaspoon salt until well-combined. Place green onions, pickles, and dill in reserved large bowl. Add potatoes to large bowl and gently toss to combine. Add sour cream mixture to bowl and toss until potatoes are fully coated. Chill for 20 to 30 minutes, or until potato salad has reached about room temperature, then garnish with more dill just before serving.

party potato salad

SERVES 10 TO 12
ACTIVE: 35 MINUTES
TOTAL: 35 MINUTES

1 pound (455 g) bacon

2½ pounds (1.2 kg) Yukon Gold potatoes, peeled and cut into 1½-inch (4-cm) pieces

1 teaspoon kosher salt, plus more for cooking potatoes

½ cup (65 g) finely chopped sweet onion (from 1 small onion)

6 green onions, thinly sliced (white and light green parts separated from dark green parts)

1½ teaspoons smoked paprika

¾ teaspoon freshly ground black pepper

½ cup (120 ml) mayonnaise, such as Duke's

¼ cup (60 ml) finely chopped sweet and spicy pickles, such as Wickles Wicked Pickle Chips

4 teaspoons pickle juice (from pickle jar)

1 teaspoon Dijon mustard

I know you might be thinking, *Isn't one potato salad recipe enough?* The answer is no. Southerners love potato salads: Some have lots of mustard, others swap mayonnaise for oil and vinegar. While creamy potato salads will always reign supreme for me, I admit that there are some instances that call for sour cream–dressed ones (see page 148). For a mayonnaise option, this Party Potato Salad will do the trick. It's my twist on the recipe I grew up eating, and it's always a hit and is one of the best potato salads out there (largely due to the bacon grease).

1. Preheat oven to 400°F (205°C). Line a rimmed baking sheet with aluminum foil. Place bacon in a single layer on prepared baking sheet. Bake in preheated oven until crisp, 20 to 25 minutes. Let bacon drain on paper towels; reserve bacon grease. (You should have about 3 tablespoons of grease.) When bacon is cool enough to handle, crumble and set aside.

2. While bacon is cooking, place potatoes in a large saucepan. Add enough water to fully submerge potatoes, season water with salt, then bring to a boil over medium-high heat. Reduce heat to medium and cook until potatoes are fork tender, 18 to 20 minutes. Drain potatoes well.

3. Meanwhile, in a large bowl, place sweet onion, white and light green parts of sliced green onions (being sure to save the dark green parts), smoked paprika, salt, and pepper. Add 3 tablespoons hot bacon grease and drained hot potatoes; toss well to coat. (The hot potatoes and bacon grease will help soften the onions and bring out the flavors of the smoked paprika.) Add mayonnaise, pickles, pickle juice, mustard, and three-quarters of the crumbled bacon to the bowl. Toss well to coat. Some of the potatoes may begin to mash—this is totally okay (and honestly my preferred way of eating potato salad). The creamier, the better, in my opinion, so keep stirring until you reach your desired consistency!

4. Transfer potato salad to a serving dish and garnish with remaining crumbled bacon and dark green parts of green onions.

lime-beer shandy
(page 55)

onion rings with kickin' ranch

SERVES 6
ACTIVE: 35 MINUTES
TOTAL: 50 MINUTES, INCLUDING RANCH DIP

1 medium sweet onion, cut crosswise into ½-inch-thick (12-mm) slices (2½ cups / 275 g)

1 cup (125 g) all-purpose flour

1 cup (240 ml) whole buttermilk

1 large egg

1½ teaspoons kosher salt, divided

2 cups (160 g) panko, divided

3 cups (720 ml) vegetable oil, for frying

Kickin' Ranch (recipe follows)

I love an onion ring, sometimes (but not always) more than a french fry. There are lots of ways to make onion rings, but this version—wet batter dipped in crispy panko breadcrumbs—is my preferred style. Best washed down with a Lime-Beer Shandy (page 55) or a glass of bubbles, these are worth bringing out the deep fryer for!

1 Separate onion slices into individual rings and place in a large bowl with flour; toss to coat onion rings evenly in flour. Transfer coated onions to a baking sheet. Add buttermilk, egg, and 1 teaspoon of the salt to flour; whisk until smooth. In a medium shallow dish, place 1 cup (80 g) panko.

2 Working in batches, dredge coated onion rings in batter, allowing excess to drip off. Then, dredge in panko; place on a wire rack. Once panko becomes too wet to coat rings, discard and place remaining 1 cup (80 g) panko in shallow dish and continue dredging. Let stand on wire rack 15 minutes before frying.

3 While onion rings stand, heat oil in a medium Dutch oven over medium-high heat to 350°F (175°C). Fry onion rings in batches until golden and crisp, about 3 minutes, turning once halfway through. Drain on wire racks and sprinkle evenly with remaining ½ teaspoon salt. Serve with Kickin' Ranch.

kickin' ranch

MAKES 1⅓ CUPS (315 ML)

1 cup (240 ml) sour cream

3 tablespoons whole buttermilk

2 tablespoons very finely chopped jalapeño (from 1 medium)

1½ tablespoons sriracha chile sauce

1 (1-ounce / 28-g) packet ranch seasoning mix

⅛ teaspoon kosher salt

I absolutely love ranch dressing. Growing up, one of my favorite restaurants was the Barbecue Pit in Moultrie, Georgia. Ask anyone who's eaten there, and they will tell you they have the world's best ranch.

This kickin' ranch does not quite live up to the Barbecue Pit ranch standard I hold so high. I don't know if I will ever be able to re-create it perfectly, but it's still a great recipe for ranch dressing with a spicy kick, best served with my onion rings (see above).

In a medium bowl, whisk all ingredients together until smooth.

hot honey–butter chicken wings

SERVES 6
ACTIVE: 20 MINUTES
TOTAL: 55 MINUTES

3½ pounds (1.6 kg) chicken wings, separated into drummettes and flats (wing tips removed, about 13 whole wings)

1 tablespoon baking powder

4¼ teaspoons kosher salt, divided

Cooking spray

¼ cup (55 g) unsalted butter

¼ cup (60 ml) hot honey, such as Red Clay

2 teaspoons hot sauce, such as Red Clay

1 small jalapeño, thinly sliced into rings (¼ cup / 40 g)

¼ cup (10 g) cilantro leaves, optional

I haven't fried a chicken wing since I learned this trick for baking crispy ones. This sauce is my definition of the perfect wing sauce: sweet, slightly spicy, and just sticky enough to warrant the need for a damp napkin when you're done.

1. Preheat oven to 450°F (230°C). Pat chicken wings very dry with paper towels and place in a large bowl. In a small bowl, stir together baking powder and 4 teaspoons of the salt, then sprinkle over chicken; toss well to coat. Line a rimmed baking sheet with parchment paper or foil, then fit a wire rack into baking sheet. Spray wire rack with cooking spray, then arrange chicken, fatty side down, in a single layer on wire rack.

2. Bake in preheated oven until crisp on one side and lightly golden, about 25 minutes. Turn chicken over and bake until well browned and crispy, 20 to 25 minutes more.

3. Meanwhile, in a small saucepan, bring butter, hot honey, hot sauce, and remaining ¼ teaspoon salt to a boil over medium-high heat. Cook for 30 seconds, then remove from heat. When chicken wings are crisp, place wings in a large bowl. Add hot honey butter sauce to bowl with jalapeño; toss well to coat wings in sauce. Transfer to a serving platter and garnish with cilantro, if using.

not your mama's broccoli salad

SERVES 8
ACTIVE: 25 MINUTES
TOTAL: 35 MINUTES

Exactly as the title suggests, this broccoli salad is not the one you grew up eating. I love old-school broccoli salad—the one with the sweet mayo-based dressing, bacon, red onions, and raisins. There really isn't anything to improve on from the original version, but this colorful twist on the classic is a delicious way to fall in love with broccoli salad all over again.

1 pound (455 g) broccoli florets, cut into bite-size pieces (6½ cups / 585 g florets)

1 tablespoon olive oil

½ teaspoon kosher salt

½ cup (360 ml) mayonnaise

2 tablespoons pickled onion liquid (from Pickled Onion recipe, page 210)

1 tablespoon granulated sugar

1 small Honeycrisp apple, cored and chopped into ½-inch (12-mm) pieces (1 cup / 180 g)

1 cup (110 g) matchstick carrots

½ cup (120 ml) Pickled Onions (page 210)

⅓ cup (50 g) golden raisins

⅓ cup (45 g) chopped roasted, salted peanuts

8 slices bacon, cooked and crumbled

1. Preheat oven to 425°F (220°C). Place broccoli in an even layer on a rimmed baking sheet. Drizzle with oil and sprinkle with salt, tossing evenly to coat. Bake in preheated oven until bright green and starting to turn lightly golden on edges, 10 to 12 minutes. Remove from oven and let cool completely on baking sheet, about 20 minutes.

2. While broccoli is cooling, in a medium bowl, whisk together mayonnaise, pickled onion liquid, and granulated sugar until smooth.

3. In a large bowl, place cooled broccoli, carrots, pickled onions, raisins, peanuts, and bacon. Pour in mayonnaise mixture and toss well to coat. Serve immediately, or refrigerate up to 4 hours before serving.

my favorite pimiento cheese

MAKES ABOUT 3 CUPS (744 G)
ACTIVE: 15 MINUTES
TOTAL: 4 HOURS 15 MINUTES

1 (8-ounce / 225-g) block sharp Cheddar cheese

1 (4-ounce / 115-g) block mild hoop Cheddar cheese

1 (4-ounce / 115-g) block creamy non-smoked Gouda cheese

1 cup (240 ml) mayonnaise, such as Duke's

2 (4-ounce / 115-g) jars sliced pimientos, drained

2 tablespoons finely grated sweet onion

1½ teaspoons Worcestershire sauce

1 teaspoon freshly ground black pepper

½ teaspoon kosher salt

¼ teaspoon cayenne pepper

¼ teaspoon smoked paprika

There are so many ways to customize pimiento cheese. The endless options for stir-ins and types of cheeses are daunting but always delicious. For me, there are a few essential ingredients I love to incorporate into every pimiento cheese:

Number one: Duke's mayonnaise, always.

Number two: Worcestershire sauce for depth of flavor.

Number three: freshly grated Vidalia or sweet onion.

After that, everything else is up to interpretation. The pimiento cheese world is your oyster. Just be sure to always shred your own cheese.

Grate all cheeses on large holes of a box grater into a large bowl; set aside. In a medium bowl, stir together mayonnaise, pimientos, onion, Worcestershire, black pepper, salt, cayenne, and smoked paprika. Fold mayonnaise mixture into cheese until very well-combined. Cover and refrigerate at least 4 hours or until ready to serve.

fried chicken sliders with pimiento cheese

SERVES 6
ACTIVE: 15 MINUTES
TOTAL: 15 MINUTES

12 slider buns or dinner rolls

My Favorite Pimiento Cheese (see page 154)

6 fried chicken tenders, halved

12 pickled okra pods, such as Wickles, halved lengthwise

I grew up watching the Masters with my grandparents, and the picturesque scenes of pink and white flowers, the sounds of golf claps and hushed announcers, and the taste of my nana's pimiento cheese fill my head every April. My pimiento cheese recipe differs from both the famous Augusta National recipe and the one Nana made, because I gussy it up with Gouda cheese, Worcestershire sauce, sweet onion, and paprika. I like to serve it on slider buns with fried chicken tenders and pickled okra, topped with toothpicks fashioned after the iconic Augusta yellow tee flag. They're so good that your guests will want to stay long after the Green Jacket ceremony ends.

Spread about ¼ cup (62 g) of pimiento cheese on bottom half of each bun. Top each with ½ fried chicken tender, 2 halves of pickled okra, and top bun half. Skewer with toothpicks to hold in place, if desired.

Tea-Time at the MASTERS®
COOKBOOK
HALL OF FAME
A Collection of Recipes · The Junior League of Augusta, Georgia
BYRDIE Golf
SOCIAL WEAR
HOLE
YARDAGE
PAR
PLAYER
Under Par
Overdressed
Scorer:
Attest:
MASTERS
R21817
2005 MASTERS
$175.00
NOT FOR RESALE
NO REFUND
Masters Club Dinner
April 9, 2024
Tapas y Pintxos
Ibericos
Idiazabal con Trufa Negra
Tortilla de Patatas
Chistorra con Patata
Lentejas Estofadas
Croqueta de Pollo
First Course
TASTE OF THE MASTERS
Sandwiches
Egg Salad
Pimento Cheese
Pork Bar B Que
Snacks
Potato Chips
Bar B Que Potato Chips
Chocolate Chip Cookies
1999
MASTERS
PRICE $100
R17575
75th MASTERS
1934 - 2011
EGG SALAD
PIMENTO CHEESE
APRIL 6,7,8,9
1995
PRICE $100
X18135
MASTERS
JOIN US TO WATCH
THE
SATURDAY, APRIL 13TH
AUGUSTA NATIONAL GOLF CLUB, AUGUSTA, GA.
MASTERS
SINCE 1934
1934
U.S.A. TOURNAMENT

masters party

serving suggestions

My favorite week of the year is when the azaleas and dogwoods are in full bloom at Augusta National Golf Club. Masters Week ranks just behind Easter and Christmas as my third favorite holiday. (It helps that it's always right before my birthday on April 16th.) And while I know that a golf tournament does not actually constitute a holiday, I like to treat it like one. The Masters is a Southern tradition, like the Kentucky Derby or Mardi Gras. For a particular contingent of the South, the four-day tournament is as big of a deal as any other major sporting event. There is a certain fanfare that makes it special: It's all about Augusta National's blooming pink azaleas, pimiento cheese sandwiches, and green jackets. Although I've never been to the tournament, I celebrate by hosting a string of get-togethers with plenty of food and drink. Regulated gameplay doesn't technically start until Thursday, but my festivities tee off on Wednesday in time for the annual Par 3 Contest. Each day, I plan a special menu inspired by classic Masters' fare.

fried summer vegetables with rosemary and honey

SERVES 6
ACTIVE: 30 MINUTES
TOTAL: 30 MINUTES

1 pound (455 g) summer squash and/or eggplant

Canola oil, for frying

1 cup (125 g) all-purpose flour

3½ teaspoons kosher salt, divided

3 cups (240 g) panko breadcrumbs, divided

3 large eggs

Flaky sea salt, such as Maldon

1½ tablespoons honey

2 tablespoons fresh rosemary leaves, for garnish

After spending a summer in southern Spain, I came to realize the culture there is similar in ways to the slower rhythms of life in the southern United States. I fell in love with the people, the culture, and the food when I was there, and now every time I visit, I feel almost like I'm going home. Inspired by one of my favorite Spanish tapas, berenjenas con miel (fried eggplant with honey), these fried summer vegetables are a taste of both my Southern homes: here and across the ocean.

1 Cut squash (if using) in half lengthwise, then slice into ¼-inch-thick (12-mm) half-moons. Set aside. Cut eggplant (if using) in half lengthwise, then cut each half in half lengthwise again. Slice eggplant quarters into ¼-inch-thick (12-mm) slices. Set aside.

2 In a large Dutch oven or deep cast-iron skillet, pour oil to a depth of 1 inch (2.5 cm) and heat oil over medium-high heat to 350°F (175°C). Adjust heat as necessary to maintain a temperature of 350°F (175°C).

3 While oil is coming to temperature, place flour in a shallow dish or pie plate with 1 teaspoon kosher salt; whisk to combine. In another shallow dish, place 1½ cups (120 g) of the panko with ¾ teaspoon kosher salt; whisk to combine. Crack eggs into a third shallow dish. Add 1 teaspoon of kosher salt and whisk well.

4 Working in batches, dredge squash and/or eggplant in the flour mixture until very lightly coated, being sure to shake off any excess flour. Dredge flour-coated vegetables in egg mixture to coat, letting any excess drip off before finally dredging in the panko mixture. Press panko mixture into vegetables to help it adhere. As panko starts to get clumpy, discard and replenish with remaining 1½ cups (120 g) panko and ¾ teaspoon kosher salt.

5 Working in 4 batches, fry vegetables at 350°F (175°C) until golden brown and crisp, 2 to 3 minutes, turning halfway through to ensure even browning. Use a spider or slotted heatproof spoon to transfer to a paper towel–lined plate or wire rack to drain. Season with a pinch of flaky salt, then continue frying remaining 3 batches of vegetables. Drain on paper towels and season with flaky salt. Transfer fried vegetables to a serving platter, drizzle with honey, and garnish with rosemary.

tip: These are really great dipped in Whipped Feta (page 181) or with Goes-on-Everything Balsamic Syrup drizzled on top (page 26).

classic deviled eggs

SERVES 6
ACTIVE: 25 MINUTES
TOTAL: 25 MINUTES

6 large eggs

Ice

1 tablespoon mayonnaise

4 teaspoons Durkee's Famous Sauce

1½ tablespoons finely chopped sweet and spicy pickles, such as Wickles Wicked Pickle Chips

¼ teaspoon kosher salt

¼ teaspoon freshly ground black pepper

Smoked paprika, for garnish (optional)

Fresh dill, for garnish (optional)

I haven't always put Durkee's Famous Sauce in my deviled eggs, but after I made a video trying out the "secret ingredient to the best-ever deviled eggs," I've never looked back. One *Southern Living* editor's grandmother swears by Durkee's in her deviled eggs, so we wrote an article about it. People went crazy for it, saying their mother or grandmother or aunt also put Durkee's in their eggs, so I knew immediately I had to try it. Though my deviled egg toppings or stir-ins might differ from party to party, the Durkee's will always remain.

1. Fill a large pot with water; bring to a boil over high heat. Carefully lower eggs into boiling water; cook, undisturbed, for 12 minutes. Meanwhile, fill a large bowl halfway with ice; add water to cover. Set ice bath aside.
2. Using a slotted spoon, immediately transfer cooked eggs from boiling water to ice bath. Let stand until completely cooled, at least 5 minutes.
3. Working with 1 egg at a time, firmly tap on a flat surface until cracks form all over the shell. Peel under cold running water.
4. Cut eggs in half lengthwise; remove yolks and place in a medium bowl. Set egg white halves aside. Using a fork, mash together yolks, mayonnaise, and Durkee's in a medium bowl. Add pickles, salt, and pepper; stir well to combine.
5. Spoon or pipe about 1 tablespoon yolk mixture into each egg white half. Garnish with smoked paprika and dill, if desired. Serve immediately, or store, covered, in refrigerator up to 3 days.

old bay rémoulade with crudités and shrimp

SERVES 8
ACTIVE: 30 MINUTES
TOTAL: 30 MINUTES

1 small garlic clove

1½ cups mayonnaise

2 tablespoons ketchup

2 teaspoons drained capers, finely chopped

2 teaspoons stone-ground mustard

2 teaspoons Worcestershire sauce

2 teaspoons prepared horseradish

1½ teaspoons Old Bay seasoning

2 pounds cooked peel 'n' eat large shrimp

8 ounces (225 g) fresh haricots verts (French green beans), trimmed and steamed

8 Persian cucumbers, quartered lengthwise

16 small carrots with tops, trimmed and halved lengthwise

16 radishes, halved if large

Growing up, I'd go to our beach house on Saint George Island, Florida, with my family. We would make the three-hour drive from Moultrie, Georgia, down to the Gulf any chance we got. As we crossed the bridge onto the island, our first stop was Doug's Fresh Seafood Market, a bright yellow trailer stocked with the best selection of fish in town. After picking up Mr. Doug's catch of the day, we'd unpack the car and head straight for the beach to soak in the last few hours of sun before dinner. Our supper always featured goodies we'd bought from the seafood truck served with a few ingredients Mama had brought from home.

My recipe for Old Bay rémoulade with crudités and shrimp is an ode to those getaways we took years ago. Stir together Old Bay seasoning, mayonnaise, and a few pantry staples for an easy sauce that tastes amazing served with steamed peel 'n' eat shrimp or any other fresh seafood. It's the perfect first-day-at-the-beach supper, which, now that I'm an adult, is ideal paired with rosé spritzers enjoyed with my friends. The rémoulade (which also travels well if kept in a cooler) can be prepared up to one week in advance; store it in an airtight container in the refrigerator until ready to serve.

1. Using the flat side of a chef's knife, smash garlic on a cutting board. Run the flat side of the knife over the garlic until a paste forms, and place the garlic paste in a medium bowl. Whisk in mayonnaise, ketchup, capers, mustard, Worcestershire, horseradish, and Old Bay until smooth. Transfer rémoulade to a serving bowl.

2. To serve, arrange bowl of rémoulade with shrimp and vegetables on a large platter. Store the rémoulade in an airtight container in the refrigerator up to 1 week.

hot brown party rolls

SERVES 6
ACTIVE: 15 MINUTES
TOTAL: 45 MINUTES

Cooking spray

1 (12-count) package small sweet Hawaiian rolls, such as King's Hawaiian

5 ounces (140 g) shredded Gruyère cheese, divided

½ pound (225 g) thinly sliced deli turkey

1 small tomato, cut into ¼-inch (6-mm) slices

6 slices thick-cut bacon, such as Wright Brand, cooked and cut into 2-inch (5-cm) pieces

¼ cup (1 ounce / 28 g) shredded Parmesan cheese

¾ cup (180 ml) melted salted butter

1 tablespoon Dijon mustard

2 teaspoons dried minced onion

1½ teaspoons Worcestershire sauce

1 teaspoon light brown sugar

½ teaspoon grated garlic (from 1 medium garlic clove)

½ teaspoon Mexican-style hot sauce, such as Cholula Hot Sauce

This is my Derby Day spin on classic ham and cheese rolls (you know the ones). These rolls go viral every time I share them on social media—and for good reason. While they are perfect for the Derby, they're also great for showers, brunches, and picnics year-round.

1 Preheat oven to 375°F (190°C). Lightly spray an 11 by 7-inch (28 by 17-cm) baking dish with cooking spray. Split rolls horizontally (without separating into individual rolls); place bottom halves of rolls in prepared baking dish.

2 Top bottom halves of rolls with half of Gruyère cheese. Add turkey slices, folding to fit evenly on Gruyère. Place tomato slices in an even layer on turkey. Top evenly with bacon pieces. Add remaining half of Gruyère in an even layer on bacon. Sprinkle evenly with Parmesan. Cover with top halves of rolls.

3 Stir together melted butter, mustard, minced onion, Worcestershire, brown sugar, garlic, and hot sauce in a 2-cup (480-ml) liquid measuring cup. Slowly pour mixture over rolls in baking dish, allowing it to soak into rolls. Cover dish with aluminum foil and bake until cheese is melted, about 15 minutes. Uncover, and continue baking until tops are golden brown and crisp, 8 to 10 minutes. Remove from oven; let stand 5 minutes before serving. Serve hot sandwiches from the baking dish.

the onion dog

SERVES AS MANY AS YOU WANT IT TO!
ACTIVE: 45 MINUTES
TOTAL: 45 MINUTES

CARAMELIZED ONIONS (MAKES ABOUT 1 CUP / 240 G):

2 teaspoons olive oil

1 medium sweet onion, thinly sliced (2 cups / 220 g slices)

½ teaspoon kosher salt

HOT DOGS AND TOPPINGS (AMOUNTS DEPEND ON HOW MANY YOU'RE SERVING):

Brioche hot dog buns, warmed

Mayonnaise

Pepper jack cheese slices (1 per bun)

Hot cooked jumbo all-beef franks (1 per bun)

Caramelized onions (see above)

Pickled Onions (page 210)

Vidalia onion relish (see note)

Thinly sliced green onions

Crispy fried onions, such as French's

This is a "no-recipe" recipe. It's meant to be a choose-your-own-adventure situation. I don't include actual measurements, because everything depends on how many people you're serving. Amounts of each topping are just a recommendation; feel free to add more or less of each one or leave a topping off completely. If you've never tried mayonnaise and cheese on a hot dog, you're missing out! Ketchup and mustard are also delicious, but in the interest of not having too many toppings, I left them off here. Feel free to use them if you'd like.

1. **Make the caramelized onions:** In a medium nonstick skillet, heat oil over medium heat. Add onions to skillet and cook, stirring occasionally, until softened, about 10 minutes. Continue to cook, stirring occasionally, being sure to prevent burning, until onions have turned a deep caramel color, about 20 more minutes. Add 1 tablespoon of water at a time, if needed, to prevent over-browning, and cook until water totally evaporates. Stir in salt, then remove from heat. Use immediately, or store in an airtight container in the refrigerator for up to 5 days. Warm before serving.

2. **To assemble hot dogs:** Spread mayonnaise in each of the warmed buns. Place a slice of cheese into each bun, then add hot cooked franks to buns. (Alternatively, place pepper jack onto beef franks during last minute of cooking to allow cheese to melt before placing in buns.) Dress hot dogs with toppings as desired.

if this isn't southern . . . Years ago in a general store in the middle-of-nowhere-Georgia, I happened upon a jar of Braswell's Vidalia Onion Relish. I bought it out of curiosity, since I love Vidalia onions and anything pickle-y in flavor. It was out of this world. I went through the jar quickly, and I couldn't seem to find it anywhere. I went to my favorite local butcher shop and market in Moultrie and asked if they could place an order for some, and they did. It became such a popular item they decided to jar up some of their own. The Joe Kem's Market Vidalia Onion Relish is now a staple item in my pantry. Anytime my parents come to visit, they know to bring a jar. Aside from hot dogs, I serve it with collard greens, pinto beans, field peas, tomatoes and rice, on charcuterie boards, in potato salads . . . just to name a few. If you're lucky enough to pass through Moultrie, do yourself a favor and head to Joe Kem's Market for a jar. Tell them I sent you!

I spent quite a few nights of my childhood standing on a stool at a plastic tablecloth–covered kitchen island helping my parents rub our signature seasoning all over Boston butts and ribs for barbecue competitions. My parents and some of their friends competed in local BBQ cook-offs as the Butts Unlimited team. (I know; the name makes me laugh too.) If you've never been to a barbecue competition, let me set the scene: Teams arrive the night before judging with coolers of seasoned meat and sauces ready for basting. They camp out all night, tending to the smoker and trying to hide their "secret" techniques from their fellow competitors. For a kid, it was incredible. We rented an RV camper—a real treat—and got to run around the camp, handing out barbecue sandwiches to anyone who asked. Butts Unlimited consistently placed in several categories, including Boston Butt, Ribs, Chicken, and Brunswick Stew. The secret to all the accolades had a little to do with the judges' tastes and a lot to do with our secret seasoning.

At the time, my mama would mix up big batches of the spice blend to use for the competitions, but since they've been out of the barbecue competition circuit for a while, my Daddy—quite the entrepreneur and someone who ALWAYS needs something to work on—decided to bottle it. My parents put it on nearly everything they cook, and lots of our friends and family have sworn by it as their own "house seasoning" for years. Though I've come up with my own House Seasoning that you can read about on page 20, when I taste anything with WayneO's Southern Seasoning on it, I immediately feel at home.

Over the years, my daddy, also known as Farmer WayneO, has given me more life lessons than I can even begin to remember. I swear the man stays up at night thinking of things to teach me. Thanks to him, I'm stubbornly independent and extra impatient. Many of his lessons stick, but try as he might, I'm not going to become the family's next pitmaster. There are no barbecue recipes in this book because I'm not patient enough to learn them (you can thank him for that), but there is one signature WayneO's Southern Seasoning recipe I have perfected: the boiled peanut. It's one of his only specialties that doesn't involve lighting a smoker, but since the majority of the recipes in this book are inspired by women in my family, I had to give one to the man who taught me *almost* everything I know.

wayne O's boiled peanuts

SERVES 8 TO 10
ACTIVE: 10 MINUTES
TOTAL: 3 TO 24 HOURS

½ to 1 cup (240 g) kosher salt

2½ pounds (265 g) raw peanuts in shell or 2½ pounds (265 g) green peanuts

½ cup (48 g) all-purpose seasoning blend, such as WayneO's Southern Seasoning

If a slow cooker is more your speed (and time is on your side), you can use one to cook your peanuts, too. Depending on the slow cooker size, you may have to reduce the amount of peanuts, salt, and water. For 1½ pounds (680 g) of peanuts, use a 6-quart slow cooker and ¼ cup all-purpose seasoning, ½ cup kosher salt, and 14 cups (3.3 L) of water. Cook on high, 10 to 12 hours, for raw, soaked peanuts, or 4 to 6 hours for green peanuts. See instructions below for soaking raw peanuts.

1. If using raw peanuts in shell, place 2 gallons (7.6 L) of water in a large, 10- to 12-quart (9.5- to 11.4-L) stockpot with ½ cup (120 g) of the salt; stir to dissolve salt. Add raw peanuts to water, then place a large dinner plate over top to help the peanuts fully submerge. Let peanuts soak 8 hours or overnight. If you are using green peanuts, you can skip this step.

2. Drain soaked raw peanuts, discarding the soaking water. Leave peanuts in pot. (Or add green peanuts to a large, 10- to 12-quart (9.5- to 11.4-L) stockpot, if you are not using soaked raw peanuts.)

3. Add 2 gallons (7.6 L) of water, all-purpose seasoning, and ½ cup (120 g) kosher salt to the pot. Bring to a boil over high heat, then reduce heat to low and simmer until peanuts are tender, 5 to 8 hours for raw peanuts or 2 to 3 hours for green peanuts. Keep adding water to pot throughout the cooking process so that peanuts are mostly submerged throughout the cooking time. Check the tenderness of your peanuts every hour or so—they should be tender, but not mushy. Taste for salt halfway through the cooking time, adding more if needed. When peanuts are cooked to your desired tenderness, turn off the heat and let them stay in the water until cooled slightly, about 30 minutes. Drain and serve warm or cooled completely. Store in the shell in an airtight container in the refrigerator for up to 10 days.

---

if this isn't southern . . . If you're passing through South Georgia on Highway 520, stop at Merritt Pecan Company for a bottle of WayneO's Southern Seasoning, or order it online at merritt-pecan.com.

whipped goat cheese with bacon jam

SERVES 8
ACTIVE: 30 MINUTES
TOTAL: 30 MINUTES

8 ounces (225 g) bacon (6 slices), chopped

1 cup (110 g) chopped sweet onion (from 1 small onion)

3 tablespoons light brown sugar

1 tablespoon water

1 teaspoon smoked paprika

½ teaspoon Worcestershire sauce

8 ounces (225 g) goat cheese, softened

4 ounces (115 g) cream cheese, softened

1 tablespoon olive oil

½ teaspoon kosher salt

Thyme leaves, for garnish

Crackers or crostini

Before I started in the *Southern Living* Test Kitchen, I worked as a line cook at a well-known restaurant in Atlanta. A popular menu item there, called Jars, consisted of a platter of toast points for dipping into jars of all sorts of dips, the crown jewel being the pimiento cheese with bacon jam. Night after night, I would grab the quarts of bacon jam from the walk-in fridge that the prep cook had made that morning and bring them to my station to be spooned over pimiento cheese once the orders started coming in. At the end of the night, there would be just enough bacon jam left over for me to snack on. After my stint at the restaurant was over, you might think I'd never want to touch bacon jam again. Emphasis on the "might"!

This recipe is creamy, smoky, crunchy, sweet, and entirely irresistible, just like my late-night restaurant snack. While I love my version with the goat cheese, it's perfectly acceptable to eat this bacon jam exactly as I did while working on the line—or as a topper to an almost endless list of dips, sandwiches, veggies, and more. However you decide to serve it, I hope it becomes a dish that you'll keep coming back to—just maybe not every single night.

1. In a 10-inch (25-cm) skillet, cook bacon over medium heat, stirring occasionally, until fat renders and bacon starts to crisp on the edges, about 9 minutes. Remove from heat. Using a slotted spoon, transfer bacon to a paper towel–lined plate. Pour drippings into a heatproof measuring cup. Add 2 tablespoons drippings back to skillet; reserve remaining drippings for another use.

2. Add onion and cooked bacon to skillet; cook over medium heat, stirring often, until onion is caramelized, about 8 minutes.

3. Stir brown sugar, water, smoked paprika, and Worcestershire into bacon mixture; cook, stirring constantly, until syrupy and combined, 15 to 30 seconds. Remove from heat; transfer mixture to a heatproof measuring cup or bowl. Let cool slightly, about 5 minutes.

4. Beat goat cheese, cream cheese, oil, and salt with an electric mixer fitted with a whisk attachment on medium speed until smooth and creamy, about 30 seconds.

5. Spread goat cheese mixture inside a shallow bowl. Top with bacon jam and garnish with thyme leaves. Serve with crackers or crostini.

pimiento queso fundido

SERVES 6
ACTIVE: 20 MINUTES
TOTAL: 20 MINUTES

2 teaspoons olive oil

1 cup (110 g) thinly sliced sweet onion (from 1 medium onion)

¼ teaspoon kosher salt

¼ teaspoon smoked paprika

3 (4-ounce / 115-g) jars sliced pimientos, well drained and patted dry, divided

2 cups (8 ounces / 225 g) shredded sharp Cheddar cheese

2 cups (8 ounces / 225 g) shredded Monterey Jack cheese

1 cup (4 ounces / 115 g) shredded Gouda cheese

1½ teaspoons Worcestershire sauce

Charred flour tortillas or chips, for serving

The only thing that can rival the devotion to our college team of choice is our love of tailgating. Because my parents set up a spread at every single University of Georgia home game during my college years, my mama's recipes quickly became touchdowns among all of my friends. She had her go-to dishes that made the roster week after week, but she was also famous for serving more out-of-the-box game-day foods, like fajitas and ravioli with marinara sauce.

Though it was never on any of her creative tailgating menus, this pimiento queso fundido (melted cheese) is inspired by my mama's love for keeping hungry college students fed on game day. Whether you make it on your stovetop at home or under a tent in your beloved college town, it's a gooey riff on pimiento cheese best served piping hot with warm tortillas or chips for dipping. True queso fundido is meant for long, melty cheese pulls—it's not like the typical queso cheese dips you're likely to get at your favorite Mexican restaurant. Be sure to have all your toppings and dippers ready to go, so that as soon as the cheese is bubbling, guests can dig in!

1. In a 10-inch (25-cm) cast-iron skillet, heat oil over medium heat. Add sliced onion. Cook, stirring often, until softened and beginning to caramelize, 8 to 9 minutes. Add salt, smoked paprika, and all but ¼ cup (96 g) of the sliced pimientos. Cook, stirring constantly, until paprika is fragrant, about 1 minute. Add Cheddar, Monterey Jack, Gouda, and Worcestershire, stirring until cheeses begin to melt. Cook, stirring occasionally, until cheeses are melted and bubbly, 5 to 7 minutes.

2. Remove skillet from heat; top mixture with remaining ¼ cup (96 g) sliced pimientos. Serve with charred tortillas and garnish with desired toppings.

some of my favorite toppings include:

EXTRA SPICY
Sliced jalapeño chiles or red Fresno chiles, crumbled cooked chorizo, and spicy corn chips (such as Fritos Flamin' Hot)

VEGGIE
Pickled red onions, charred corn kernels, diced fresh tomatoes, diced fresh bell peppers, chopped green onions, and cilantro

FULLY LOADED
Crumbled cooked bacon, crumbled queso fresco (fresh Mexican cheese), crispy fried onions, sliced pickled jalapeños, and chopped green onions

vidalia onion dip

MAKES ABOUT 2 CUPS (480 ML)
ACTIVE: 30 MINUTES
TOTAL: 40 MINUTES

2 tablespoons extra-virgin olive oil

2½ cups chopped sweet onion (from 2 medium onions)

1 teaspoon kosher salt, divided

¼ teaspoon garlic powder

¼ teaspoon freshly ground black pepper, plus more for garnish

¼ teaspoon fresh thyme leaves, plus more for garnish

1 (8-ounce / 226-g) package cream cheese, softened

½ cup (120 ml) sour cream

½ teaspoon Worcestershire sauce

Wavy kettle-cooked potato chips, for serving

These three dips make frequent appearances at my parties because they're easy, can be made ahead, and everyone loves them. The peach salsa is best for summer parties, when peaches and tomatoes are at their ripest, though mango is also a great substitute when peaches are hard to come by. Whipped feta is so easy, you'd be silly NOT to make it. And this book wouldn't be complete without an onion dip recipe, because onion dip is, objectively, the best dip in the world.

1 In a medium skillet, heat oil over medium heat. Add onion and cook, stirring occasionally, until translucent and tender, about 8 minutes. Reduce heat to medium-low, add ¼ teaspoon salt to onions, and continue cooking, stirring occasionally, until onions turn a deep golden caramel color, about 8 more minutes. If onions begin to brown quickly, add water, 1 tablespoon at a time, stirring to loosen any browned bits on bottom of skillet. When onions are caramelized, add garlic powder, pepper, and thyme to skillet. Cook 1 minute, then remove from heat and let cool 10 minutes.

2 In a medium bowl, stir together cooled onion mixture, cream cheese, sour cream, Worcestershire, and remaining ¾ teaspoon salt until well-combined. Transfer to a serving bowl and garnish with freshly ground black pepper and thyme. Serve with kettle-cooked potato chips. Store onion dip in an airtight container in the refrigerator for up to 3 days.

peach salsa

MAKES ABOUT 2 CUPS (480 ML)
ACTIVE: 15 MINUTES
TOTAL: 15 MINUTES

2 medium peaches, peeled and cut into ¼-inch (6-mm) pieces (1 cup / 155 g chopped peaches)

½ cup (75 g) multicolored cherry tomatoes, quartered

¼ cup (35 g) finely chopped red onion (from 1 small onion)

1 small jalapeño, seeded and finely chopped (2 tablespoons chopped)

1½ tablespoons finely chopped fresh cilantro

¼ teaspoon lime zest (from 1 lime)

1 teaspoon fresh lime juice (from 1 lime)

½ teaspoon honey

½ teaspoon kosher salt

In a medium bowl, combine all ingredients together; stir well to incorporate. Serve immediately or chill until ready to serve, up to 1 day in advance.

whipped feta

MAKES ABOUT 2 CUPS (480 ML)
ACTIVE: 10 MINUTES
TOTAL: 10 MINUTES

1 (8-ounce / 225 g) block feta cheese

½ cup (120 ml) plain Greek yogurt or sour cream

1 medium garlic clove, minced

1 tablespoon extra-virgin olive oil

½ teaspoon kosher salt

Grilled naan or crudités, for serving

GARNISHES:

Olive oil

Honey

Red pepper flakes

Black pepper

Thyme

Marcona almonds

Break feta into large chunks, then place in the bowl of a food processor or blender with yogurt, garlic, olive oil, and salt. Process until smooth, 1 to 2 minutes. Transfer to a serving bowl and garnish with desired toppings. Serve with grilled naan or veggies.

tip: This is also great served with my Fried Summer Vegetables on page 162.

bulldog candy

MAKES 1 CUP (150 G)
ACTIVE: 25 MINUTES
TOTAL: 40 MINUTES

2½ cups (12 ounces / 340 g) jalapeños, thinly sliced

1 Fresno chile, chopped

½ cup (110 g) packed light brown sugar

1½ teaspoons apple cider vinegar

½ teaspoon kosher salt

My tailgates are never complete without my mama's bulldog candy. Because all "damn good dawgs" have to have at least one tailgating item named after our beloved football team, "bulldog candy" is simply our family's nickname for candied jalapeños. Serve with a block of cream cheese and crackers, or use it as a condiment for pimiento cheese, burgers, hot dogs, or as an accoutrement for a charcuterie board. I also love it as a topper for my guacamole with pork rinds (recipe follows).

In a small saucepan, bring all ingredients to a boil over medium-high heat, stirring occasionally. Reduce heat to medium-low and cook until jalapeños have turned dark in color and all sugar has turned into a very thick syrup, about 15 minutes. Transfer to a glass jar and let cool to room temperature before storing in the refrigerator for up to 10 days.

guacamole with pork rinds

SERVES 6
ACTIVE: 15 MINUTES
TOTAL: 15 MINUTES

1½ pounds (600 g) ripe avocados, halved, peeled, and seeded

4 teaspoons fresh lime juice (from 1 large lime)

¼ cup (35 g) finely chopped sweet onion (from 1 small onion)

1 large jalapeño, seeded and finely chopped (2 tablespoons)

1 tablespoon finely chopped fresh cilantro

1 teaspoon kosher salt

¼ teaspoon grated fresh garlic (from 1 large clove)

⅛ teaspoon ground cumin

½ teaspoon white wine vinegar (optional, see note)

Pork rinds, for serving

1. In a medium bowl, place avocado halves and lime juice. Use a potato masher to lightly mash avocado into large chunks. Add onion, jalapeño, cilantro, salt, garlic, cumin, and vinegar (if using) to bowl.
2. Use the potato masher to stir and mash guacamole to desired consistency. I prefer my guacamole on the chunkier side, but some people prefer smoother, so keep on mashing if that's you! Serve immediately with pork rinds.

note: If you don't have white wine vinegar on hand, just use an extra ½ teaspoon lime juice instead! It's nice to have, but not crucial!

BESIT
CON
Guava con Ch
NATURAL SODA
12 oz | 355 mL

corn-and-smoked sausage nachos

SERVES 6
ACTIVE: 30 MINUTES
TOTAL: 30 MINUTES

1 pound (4 cups / 455 g) hickory-smoked sausage, such as Conecuh, cut into ½-inch (12-mm) pieces

1½ cups (220 g) fresh yellow corn kernels (from 3 ears)

1 cup (110 g) chopped sweet onion (from 1 small onion)

¼ teaspoon kosher salt

2 teaspoons Creole seasoning, divided

1 (8-ounce / 226-g) package cream cheese, softened

½ cup half-and-half

8 ounces (225 g) thick tortilla chips or wavy kettle-cooked potato chips

1 small jalapeño chile, finely chopped

1 green onion, thinly sliced (1 tablespoon)

Unless my Dawgs are playing, I don't really care to be glued to the TV during football season. Like any good Southerner, I want the SEC to beat everyone else, but I'll gladly volunteer to be in charge of the game-time snacks if Georgia's not playing. Game-watching at home provides certain advantages to tented tailgates. At home, I can sneak to the kitchen to whip up a last-minute dish while hungry fans are happily grazing away at pregame snacks.

Best served hot off the stove, these corn-and-smoked sausage nachos will be gobbled up before the end of the first quarter. Inspired by my mama's jalapeño popper dip, a creamy and flavorful corn-studded cheese sauce covers crunchy tortilla chips, topped with the South's favorite smoked sausage. While any chip will do the trick for these nachos, my mama swears by a potato chip for any dip that includes a base of cream cheese and sweet onions. The tang of the cream cheese and the sweetness of the onions pair perfectly with a salty kettle-cooked spud.

1. Heat a large cast-iron skillet over medium-high heat. Add sausage and cook, stirring occasionally, until browned, about 8 minutes. Transfer sausage to a paper towel–lined plate using a slotted spoon; set aside. Reserve 2 tablespoons of drippings in skillet; discard remaining drippings.

2. Add corn, onion, salt, and 1½ teaspoons of the Creole seasoning to drippings in skillet; cook, stirring occasionally, until vegetables are tender, 5 to 8 minutes. Add cream cheese and half-and-half, stirring until cream cheese melts, about 1 minute. Immediately remove from heat.

3. Place chips on a platter or in a skillet. Spoon corn mixture evenly over chips; top evenly with reserved sausage, jalapeño, and green onion. Sprinkle evenly with remaining ½ teaspoon Creole seasoning. Serve immediately.

if this isn't southern . . . I am a big fan of two Southern sausage makers whose products pack loads of distinctive flavor into recipes like this one. Look for smoked sausage made by Conecuh Sausage in Evergreen, Alabama, and Stripling's General Store, based in Cordele, Georgia, and you'll become a fan too.

GEORGIA
SIC EM
SOUTH SKYSUITE
04
70
VANDERBILT UNIVERSITY
DOOLEY FIELD AT SANFORD STADIUM
SUITE
S403
TICKET
4

game-day tailgate

serving suggestions

My parents know how to throw a mean tailgate. During my four years at the University of Georgia, they made the four-hour statewide haul from our hometown of Moultrie to Athens for every home game to put on a tailgate for me and my friends. These tailgates were always elaborate. Mama knows how to pull out all the stops when it comes to decor and food, while Daddy keeps everyone entertained with oversized Jenga, cornhole, and jokes by the grill. I know the amount of work and prep they put into each weekend was intense, but it was remembered and so appreciated by everyone who stopped by. Ten years later, my friends will still stop by our old tailgating spot just to see if my parents are there. I learned everything I know about how to throw a game-watching party from the two of them. Whether your game day is on campus or streamed live in your living room, these recipes and tips are 100% WayneO and SabO–approved!

GAM
IME

chicken nugget–sauce pizza

SERVES 4
ACTIVE: 30 MINUTES
TOTAL: 50 MINUTES

1 pound (455 g) bakery refrigerated pizza dough

1 tablespoon, plus 1½ teaspoons extra-virgin olive oil, divided

1 small red onion, thinly sliced

⅛ teaspoon kosher salt

¼ cup (60 ml) creamy honey mustard barbecue sauce, such as Chick-fil-A, plus more for serving

1½ cups (167 g) shredded Mexican blend cheese, divided

1 cup (195 g) tightly packed cooked, shredded chicken breast (or one 12-count order chicken nuggets, chopped)

GARNISHES:

Sweet and sour sauce, such as Chick-fil-A Polynesian

5 slices bacon, cooked and crumbled

2 green onions, thinly sliced

1 small jalapeño, thinly sliced (optional)

This recipe is dedicated to my first friend, my ride-or-die, my cousin Kari. She loves a condiment more than anyone I know and gets especially excited when I tell her I've found a new way to use everyone's favorite drive-thru chicken nugget sauce . . . the fact that it involves pizza? In her eyes, I might as well be the world's best chef. Love you, KK!

1 Take pizza dough out of the refrigerator and let come to room temperature, about 30 minutes. Meanwhile, preheat oven to 425°F (220°C). In a 12-inch (30.5 cm) cast-iron skillet, heat 1 teaspoon oil over medium heat. Add red onion and cook, stirring occasionally, until soft, 6 to 8 minutes. Season with salt; remove from skillet and set aside. Wipe out skillet. (While the pizza dough is coming to room temperature, go ahead and cook your bacon if you haven't already.)

2 When pizza dough is fully at room temperature, shape dough into a 12-inch (30.5-cm) circle. Drizzle 1 tablespoon oil into skillet, covering bottom and sides of skillet with oil. Place dough into skillet, being sure to pull the dough 1 inch (2.5 cm) up the sides of the skillet for the crust. Drizzle remaining ½ teaspoon oil over dough, then prick dough all over with a fork. Bake in preheated oven about 9 minutes, or until lightly golden on top. Remove from oven and poke any air bubbles down with a fork.

3 Spread creamy honey mustard barbecue sauce evenly over prebaked crust. Top with 1 cup (112 g) of the cheese, then top with chicken and cooked red onions. Top with remaining ½ cup (55 g) cheese. Return skillet to oven and continue cooking until cheese is melted and crust is golden brown, about 10 more minutes. Remove pizza from oven and drizzle with more nugget sauce and sweet and sour sauce, then top with crumbled bacon, green onions, and jalapeños, if using. Cut into 8 slices to serve.

ivy's take! Pizza night happens often at our house. A few years ago, I gave Luis a wood-fired pizza oven for his birthday, though I have to admit I definitely bought it for myself, too. While we can never go wrong with classic pepperoni, our most-loved pizza creations have come out of getting creative with ingredients in our fridge, Chicken Nugget–Sauce Pizza being our shining star. When we're planning on pizza night, I love to make a batch of Bulldog Candy (page 182) to top our pizzas and Roasted Garlic Butter (page 24) for dipping our crust.

loaded mac 'n' cheese

SERVES 4 AS A MAIN OR 8 AS A SIDE
ACTIVE: 30 MINUTES
TOTAL: 45 MINUTES

5 tablespoons (71 g) salted butter, divided

1 cup (110 g) chopped sweet onion (from 1 medium onion)

1 cup (145 g) fresh corn kernels, any color (from 2 cobs)

1 (4-ounce / 113-g) can diced green chiles, drained

1 (4-ounce / 113-g) jar diced pimientos, drained

1 tablespoon minced fresh garlic (from 3 medium cloves)

½ teaspoon smoked paprika

3 tablespoons all-purpose flour

2 cups (480 ml) whole milk

4 ounces (115 g) cream cheese, cubed

1 block sharp Cheddar cheese (8 ounces / 225 g), shredded (2 cups), divided

1 block Colby Jack cheese (8 ounces / 225 g), shredded (2 cups), divided

½ cup (120 ml) mayonnaise

¾ teaspoon kosher salt

12 ounces (340 g) medium or large pasta shells, cooked in salted water according to package directions

1 cup (80 g) panko bread crumbs

6 slices bacon (84 g), cooked and crumbled (¾ cup)

3 small green onions (15 g), thinly sliced (¼ cup)

There are lots of ways to go about making macaroni and cheese, but the two main categories a recipe can fall into are stovetop or baked. I prefer stovetop versions, because I like how the cheese sauce gets stuck in the crevices of the pasta. For an extra-creamy sauce, I like to add in a secret ingredient—mayonnaise. It can be our little secret—it's on you if you tell your guests.

1. Preheat oven to 400°F / 205°C). In a 12-inch (30.5 cm) cast-iron skillet, cook 3 tablespoons of the butter over medium heat until melted. Add sweet onion to skillet and cook, stirring occasionally, until they begin to turn translucent, about 6 minutes. Add corn to skillet and continue cooking for 2 minutes, or until onion is softened. Add green chiles, pimientos, garlic, and smoked paprika to skillet and cook until fragrant, about 1 minute.

2. Stir in flour and cook until raw flour smell is gone and flour begins to smell slightly nutty, about 2 minutes. Slowly whisk in milk and cook, stirring constantly, until mixture has thickened, 2 to 3 minutes. Stir in cream cheese and cook until melted, about 2 minutes. Turn heat to medium-low, then stir in 1½ cups (170 g) of the Cheddar and 1½ cups (170 g) of the Colby Jack. Cook, stirring constantly, until melted. Remove from heat, then stir in mayonnaise and salt.

3. Fold cooked, drained pasta shells into cheese sauce, stirring with a spatula or wooden spoon to fully coat all shells. Top pasta with remaining ½ cup (55 g) Cheddar and ½ cup (55 g) Colby Jack.

4. In a microwave-safe bowl, melt remaining 2 tablespoons butter on high in the microwave, about 30 seconds. In a medium bowl, stir together melted butter and panko until panko is coated in butter. Spread panko mixture in an even layer over the pasta in the skillet.

5. Bake in preheated oven until panko is golden brown, 10 to 15 minutes. Remove from oven and sprinkle with crumbled bacon and green onions. Let sit 5 minutes before serving.

best-ever brownies

SERVES 9
ACTIVE: 15 MINUTES
TOTAL: 2 HOURS, 15 MINUTES

Cooking spray

1 cup (225 g) salted butter

1 cup (200 g) granulated sugar

1 cup (220 g) dark brown sugar

1½ cups (11 ounces / 310 g) semisweet chocolate chunks or chips, divided

¾ cup (70 g) Dutch-process cocoa powder

2 teaspoons vanilla extract

½ teaspoon kosher salt

3 large eggs

1¼ cups (155 g) all-purpose flour

Flaky sea salt, such as Maldon, for garnish

When I was in kindergarten, the teacher asked all of the students to raise their hands and volunteer for something to bring to the class Christmas party. When I didn't raise my hand, she asked me why. I replied, "I can't bring anything because Mama burns slice-and-bake cookies." So, my teacher called my mom and told her that we could be in charge of the paper products for the party. Needless to say, Mama was mortified. But her baking skills have improved dramatically, especially for making boxed Ghirardelli brownies—which will forever be my favorite because they remind me of her. My recipe for the best-ever brownies is called the "best-ever" because they're just as good as my favorite boxed mix. The only thing that would ever be better would be making them with your mama.

1. Preheat oven to 350°F (175°C). Coat an 8-inch (20-cm) square (2-inch / 5-cm deep) metal baking pan with cooking spray. Line with parchment paper, leaving about 2 inches (5 cm) overhanging on two opposing sides of pan. Coat parchment paper with cooking spray; set aside.

2. In a medium saucepan, melt butter over medium-low heat. Once melted, whisk in granulated sugar and brown sugar until smooth, about 1 minute.

3. Remove from heat and whisk in 1 cup (206 g) of the chocolate chunks until melted. Whisk in cocoa powder, vanilla, and salt. Let cool 5 minutes.

4. Working quickly to avoid cooking eggs, crack 1 of the eggs into chocolate mixture and whisk vigorously until incorporated. Repeat with remaining eggs.

5. Fold in flour and remaining ½ cup (104 g) chocolate chunks until just combined and no dry streaks remain.

6. Pour batter into prepared baking pan and spread into an even layer.

7. Bake in preheated oven until slightly risen and top appears shiny, 35 to 38 minutes. Remove from oven, sprinkle with flaky sea salt, and cool completely in pan on a wire rack, about 1½ hours.

pumpkin whoopie pies

MAKES 14 PIES
ACTIVE: 20 MINUTES
TOTAL: 1 HOUR

PIES:

3 cups (375 g) all-purpose flour

1 teaspoon ground cinnamon

1 teaspoon pumpkin pie spice

1 teaspoon baking soda

½ teaspoon kosher salt

1 cup (220 g) packed light brown sugar

1 cup (200 g) granulated sugar

1 cup (240 ml) canola oil

1 (15-ounce / 425-g) can pure pumpkin puree

2 large eggs

1 teaspoon vanilla extract

CREAM CHEESE FILLING:

1 (8-ounce / 225-g) package cream cheese, at room temperature

½ cup (115 g) salted butter, at room temperature

1 (16-ounce / 453-g) package powdered sugar

⅛ teaspoon ground cinnamon

½ teaspoon vanilla extract

Fall doesn't start at my house until I make pumpkin whoopie pies. When I made my first batch of them in college, they were an immediate hit with my friends, and they've since become an annual tradition to kick off the fall. There's one caveat though: I will only make them in October. It's a rule I made mostly to keep myself in check from eating too many. I love making them for friends, but since it's one of my most-requested recipes, it quickly becomes a slippery slope of endless amounts of whoopies in my fridge. They are best served cold (trust me—way better than room temp) and will last, refrigerated, about a week—if you don't eat them all first.

1 **For the pies:** Preheat oven to 350°F (175°C). In a large bowl, whisk together flour, cinnamon, pumpkin pie spice, baking soda, and salt; set aside.

2 In a large bowl, with an electric mixer, beat brown sugar, granulated sugar, oil, and pumpkin on medium speed until well-combined, about 1 minute. Beat in eggs one at a time, beating well after each addition; stir in vanilla. Gradually beat in flour mixture on low speed until just combined.

3 Transfer mixture to a large piping bag or zip-top plastic bag fitted with a medium round tip. Pipe batter in 2-inch (5-cm) circles 2 inches (5 cm) apart on two parchment-lined baking sheets.

4 Bake in preheated oven for 11 minutes, or until tops are set, rotating baking sheets halfway through baking time. Let cool on baking sheets for 5 minutes, then transfer to a wire rack to cool completely, about 30 minutes.

5 **For the cream cheese filling:** In a large bowl, with an electric mixer, beat cream cheese and butter on medium speed until smooth. Gradually beat in powdered sugar on low speed until smooth, about 1 minute. Stir in cinnamon and vanilla.

6 Place frosting in a large piping bag or zip-top bag fitted with a medium round tip. Pipe frosting onto the flat side of half of the cookies. Top frosting with another cookie to create whoopie pies. Serve immediately, or chill overnight. Store in the refrigerator up to 4 days.

cast-iron s'mores dip

SERVES 8
ACTIVE: 10 MINUTES
TOTAL: 10 MINUTES

1 (12-ounce / 340-g) bag semisweet or milk chocolate chips

2 tablespoons salted butter

1 (12-ounce / 340-g) bag large marshmallows

Graham crackers, for serving

When it's not quite pumpkin whoopie season, cast-iron s'mores dip is my go-to party dessert. In fact, it's also one of my easy-to-whip-up weeknight desserts, for when the sweet tooth strikes and I need a chocolate fix.

1 Place oven rack in upper-third portion of oven, then preheat oven to broil on high. In a 10-inch (25-cm) cast-iron skillet, cook chocolate chips and butter over medium-low heat, stirring occasionally, until almost completely melted, about 3 minutes.

2 Place marshmallows in a single layer over melted chocolate. Broil in preheated oven until marshmallows are golden and toasted, 2 to 4 minutes. Serve immediately with graham crackers.

chapter 6

lazy sundays

I usually reserve my longer, more intensive recipes for Sunday afternoons. After church, we like to either go out for lunch or come home to make a quick meal, then we spend the rest of the day getting things ready for the week ahead. Sometimes that includes laundry and meal prep, sometimes it means spending a little extra time in the garden or flower beds, and sometimes it means going to the pool, because the only thing that will get us through the upcoming week is a little rest and some sunshine. Even if the afternoon's activities involve a nap, I still always end up in the kitchen. Sundays are my days to take a little extra time to savor it all.

The recipes in this chapter are meant to be made on lazy Sundays, or just on days when you've got a little more time to spend in the kitchen. There are a few scattered throughout that could probably be made as part of a weeknight dinner, but if you do decide to attempt that feat, just remember I warned you not to make the rest of your meal too intensive. As much as I want y'all to try every recipe in this book, trust me when I say after work on a Thursday is not the time to bring out the cake pans and deep fryer. (I tried it when I was developing the recipes.)

While the rest of the book mostly features my spins on Southern classics, this chapter exists to show that sometimes, the classics shouldn't be messed with. In a book called *My Southern Kitchen*, I'd be remiss not to include some old-school recipes for a few of my favorite Southern delicacies, like fried catfish, biscuits, creamed corn, and layer cakes.

You'll find my go-to roasted chicken recipe on page 224, which can double as meal prep and Sunday dinner. On page 223 you'll discover the only way you should be frying okra. You can go down a lost-layer-cakes-of-the-South rabbit hole on pages 246 and 249, or totally rethink the way you make cornbread on page 219. So many of the people I love most inspired recipes in this chapter, so I hope during one of your own lazy Sundays, you'll take the time to read through the stories I've shared about them here. Though most of the recipes in this chapter aren't ones I make often, they're all little reminders that when you do take time to stop and savor, you'll never regret it.

biscuit bowl biscuits

MAKES 12
ACTIVE: 20 MINUTES
TOTAL: 35 MINUTES

¼ cup (50 g) vegetable shortening, at room temperature, plus more for greasing pan

1 (2-pound / 907-g) package enriched bleached self-rising flour, such as White Lily

1 cup (240 ml) whole buttermilk

There are a lot of similarities in recipes for biscuits, fried chicken, and barbecue in the South. For starters, they're typically not written out, but instead passed down through memories shared with loved ones in the kitchen or around the smoker. Second, there isn't one recipe that gives the definitive right way to make biscuits, fried chicken, or barbecue because the variations on these recipes are often so vastly different. And third, most every Southerner's preferred recipe is chosen because it's the way they grew up eating it. For my daddy, there is only one way to make a biscuit. Soft, fluffy, and almost cake-like in crumb, the type he likes is very different from the buttery, flaky, crunchy-top biscuits that are so popular in modern brunch joints. He remembers his grandfather gently incorporating shortening, buttermilk, and salt into a giant wooden bowl of flour. Like magic, the buttermilk and shortening would cling to the perfect amount of flour needed to make the dough, leaving the rest of the flour completely dry. The flour that remained in the bowl was covered with a towel and set atop a cabinet for the next biscuit making day. I'm now the keeper of my great-great-grandfather's wooden biscuit bowl that was hand-carved and passed down from the carver to his son, then from my great-grandfather to his grandson, and now from my dad to me. Over the years, flour has left the scene, and now the bowl is mostly used as a catch-all or a serving piece. It's weathered, cracked, and stained, but on those days when I need something to sop up a taste of home, I pull out the bowl that knows just what to do.

1. Preheat oven to 500°F (260°C). Grease a small or medium (no smaller than 8-inch / 20-cm) round cast-iron griddle pan or skillet with shortening. Place flour in a large bowl. Spoon 2½ cups of the flour into a sifter; sift flour back into bowl. Using the back of your hand, create a nestlike shape in flour in center of bowl, pressing and packing flour down firmly.

2. Pour buttermilk directly into nest. Add shortening to buttermilk. Squeeze together shortening and buttermilk, using one hand to incorporate until no large pieces remain. Using a circular motion with your hands, gradually begin incorporating flour from sides of bowl into buttermilk mixture, working as quickly and gently as you can and incorporating only as much flour as needed until a soft dough forms. (You will not need to

continued

use all the flour in the bowl.) The dough should be soft but not wet, and it can be a bit sticky. Reserve remaining flour in bowl for flouring and, if desired, for another batch of biscuits.

3 Flour your hands, and transfer dough to a lightly floured work surface. Pat dough to about 1-inch (2.5-cm) thickness. Using a 2-inch (5-cm) biscuit cutter, cut out 8 biscuits, flouring cutter after each cutting. Reroll dough scraps and pat to 1-inch (2.5-cm) thickness. Cut remaining 4 biscuits using floured cutter. Discard any remaining scraps.

4 Arrange biscuits as close together as possible (they should be touching) on prepared griddle pan. Bake in preheated oven until tops are golden, 10 to 12 minutes. Cool 5 minutes before serving.

---

ivy's take! Super soft and fluffy, these biscuits are the no-frills, old-school biscuits my daddy grew up eating. If you've ever had a biscuit from Cracker Barrel, this is what these biscuits are like. I love the tang of the buttermilk. They're just salty enough, but still not *salty*, so you can add softened salted butter for that perfect bite. This is the kind of biscuit I want to use to sop up gravy with my cube steak, or slather with butter and pear preserves to eat alongside my breakfast. Other, sturdier biscuits are better for sandwiches or other uses, but I view these almost like I do a yeast roll—as an accompaniment to the meal, since they're super soft and small.

ening. Beat just
teaspoonfuls into ini-
brown lightly on both
and around initials, mak-
ed size. Brown on both
up. Yield: 1 dozen.
Alisa Jordan
Griffin FHA, Griffin
FFLES
en
ugar
milk
c. self-rising flour
p. oil
c. cornmeal
bine egg and sugar in bowl; mix well. Add
/4 cups milk; mix well. Add flour; stir until
oistened. Stir in oil. Add cornmeal; mix well
Add enough remaining milk to make batter
pouring consistency. Pour 1/4 at a time onto
hot 10-inch waffle iron. Bake using waffle iron
directions. Yield: 4 servings.
Jean Odom
Glennville FHA, Glennville

the georgia FHA crispy cornmeal waffle

SERVES 4
ACTIVE: 25 MINUTES
TOTAL: 25 MINUTES

1 large egg

1 tablespoon granulated sugar

1¾ cups (420 ml) whole milk

1¾ cups (220 g) self-rising flour

¼ cup (35 g) plain yellow cornmeal

¼ teaspoon kosher salt

3 tablespoons canola oil

Salted butter, softened, for serving

Warm maple syrup, for serving

This recipe comes from Jean Odom and can be found in the Georgia Future Homemakers of America cookbook *Favorite Recipes with Georgia on My Mind*. Though we have the same last name, I don't think I'm related to Jean (though one can never be too sure). Her recipe for crispy cornmeal waffles is the only one my mama makes. Something about the addition of just a little bit of cornmeal makes these special. Mama would always make a double batch to freeze, and if I was helping her, I'd throw some chocolate chips into the batter for extra fun. Frozen waffles reheat perfectly in the toaster for a quick and easy breakfast—one I reach for often when I want a taste of home.

1. Heat a waffle iron (any style will do) until hot. In a large bowl, whisk together egg and sugar until sugar is almost dissolved and egg is light in color. Whisk in milk until smooth. Add flour, cornmeal, and salt; whisk until just combined. Stir in oil.

2. Cook waffles according to waffle iron manufacturer's instructions. (This makes 4 to 6 waffles, depending on waffle iron.) Serve with butter and warm maple syrup.

note: All waffle irons are different. Some have a temperature gauge and others, like mine, just have a red and green light indicator telling you if the waffle is ready or not. You might need to run your waffles through your iron's cooking cycle one time, or maybe two, depending on how hot your iron cooks. Just keep an eye on them and take them out when they're at your desired level of crispiness.

pickled onions

MAKES 2 CUPS (480 ML)
ACTIVE: 10 MINUTES
TOTAL: 8 HOURS, 40 MINUTES

Pickled onions are great on so many things. Salads, sandwiches, tacos, and soups are all made better with a little pickled punch. Even when I eat up the last of the onions, I save the pickling liquid to use in dressings or marinades. Flip to page 153 for another way to use the pickled pink prize.

¾ cup (180 ml) red wine vinegar

¾ cup (180 ml) tap water

3 tablespoons granulated sugar

1 teaspoon kosher salt

1 medium red onion, thinly sliced

In a medium saucepan, bring vinegar, water, sugar, and salt to a boil over medium-high heat, 5 to 7 minutes. Whisk to dissolve sugar and salt. Remove from heat. Place onion slices in a 4-cup (960-ml) heatproof liquid measuring cup or medium bowl; pour hot liquid over onions. Let cool to room temperature, about 30 minutes. Cover and refrigerate at least 8 hours, or up to 10 days.

nana's marinated peas (page 212)

sweet heat garden pickles

MAKES FOUR 1-PINT (180-ML) JARS
ACTIVE: 25 MINUTES
TOTAL: 9 HOURS, 25 MINUTES

7½ ounces (215 g) radishes, small radishes left whole and large radishes cut in half (from 1 medium bunch)

6 ounces (170 g) asparagus, trimmed to 5-inch (12-cm) pieces

6 ounces (170 g) whole small carrots, cut in half lengthwise (from 1 medium bunch)

6 ounces (170 g) haricots verts (French green beans), trimmed to 5-inch (12-cm) pieces

2 large jalapeños, thinly sliced

2 teaspoons black peppercorns

2 teaspoons mustard seeds

2 teaspoons crushed red pepper

2¾ cups (660 ml) white vinegar

1½ cups (360 ml) water

1 cup (200 g) granulated sugar

3½ tablespoons kosher salt

I love a good pickle. Dill, bread and butter, spicy, you name it. This recipe is about as easy as you're going to find for pickle making. There's no fussy equipment involved, plus there are two flavor variations, since I can't decide if sweet or garlicky pickles are better. Try them both and you can be the judge.

1 Place radishes, asparagus, carrots, and haricots verts in 4 separate pint jars. Evenly divide jalapeño slices, peppercorns, mustard seeds, and crushed red pepper among jars. In a medium saucepan, heat white vinegar, water, sugar, and salt over medium-high heat. Cook, stirring often, until sugar is completely dissolved, about 5 minutes. Pour hot liquid evenly into jars.

2 Cover jars with lids and bands; cool completely to room temperature, about 1 hour. Transfer to refrigerator and chill at least overnight or up to 2 weeks.

ivy's take! To make garlicky garden pickles, omit jalapeños, reduce sugar to ½ cup (100 g), and add 3 smashed garlic cloves and 1 tablespoon fresh dill (1 large sprig) to each jar. Pour liquid into jars as directed.

nana's marinated peas

MAKES ABOUT 5 CUPS
ACTIVE: 20 MINUTES
TOTAL: 1 HOUR, 20 MINUTES

1 cup (200) granulated sugar

¾ cup (180 ml) apple cider vinegar

⅓ cup (75 ml) vegetable oil

1 (15-ounce / 425-g) can very young small, sweet peas, such as Le Sueur, drained and rinsed

1 (11-ounce / 312-g) can white shoepeg corn, drained and rinsed

1 (4-ounce / 113-g) jar diced pimientos

1 cup (145 g) finely chopped green bell pepper (from 1 small pepper)

1 cup (125 g) finely chopped sweet onion (from 1 small onion)

⅓ cup (35 g) finely chopped celery (from 1 large stalk)

1 teaspoon kosher salt

½ teaspoon freshly ground black pepper

Fresh dill and/or parsley, for serving

Growing up, we didn't serve our Thanksgiving meal on fancy china at a table set with a beautiful centerpiece, nor did we go around the room saying what we were thankful for. If you were invited to our feast, you'd walk into a room bursting at the seams with people. Everyone lined up, waiting impatiently for their turn to fill Chinet plates with food from a sea of precariously parked CorningWare and Pyrex dishes. Among the brown and beige-hued classics—dressing, potatoes, casseroles—there would be an occasional green vegetable, which would most definitely be slow cooked and swimming in a pool of pork jowl–laden pot likker.

Our potluck meal may have been fuss-free, but our cooking skills were over-the-top. There would be deep-fried turkey, lacy cornbread, and a sideboard of layer cakes and pies. Each person's signature dish could rival the next, but for me, the crown jewel of our buffet was my nana's marinated peas. Perched unassumingly alongside cooked-to-death side dishes, Nana's peas were a welcomed addition of texture, freshness, tang, and color. On their own, and often served from a repurposed Country Crock tub, the peas are just a mixture of canned and fresh vegetables dressed in a sweet, vinegar-and-oil mixture. But Nana always has known a thing or two about the proper way to eat a good plate of Southern food. The way she fixes herself a bite, perfectly stacking the peas on top of every forkful of creamy casserole or wilted greens before popping it into her mouth, is pure magic. She knows that when the peas are paired with what's on the rest of the plate, everything really comes to life. If we were a family that went around the room and said what we were thankful for, I'd give thanks for Nana's marinated peas and the lesson they've taught me on seasoning with a little tang and a lot of love.

1. In a small saucepan, combine sugar, vinegar, and oil over medium heat and cook undisturbed until sugar is dissolved, about 6 minutes. Transfer mixture to a heatproof bowl to cool, about 15 minutes.

2. In a large bowl, combine peas, corn, pimientos, bell pepper, onion, celery, salt, and black pepper. Add vinegar mixture and toss to coat. Chill at least 1 hour or up to 3 days before serving. Serve vegetables with vinegar mixture, garnished with fresh dill and/or parsley.

THE ORIGINAL
SINCE 1882
CURIOUS CRYSTALS
TRADE MARK
OF UNUSUAL PURITY
Maldon
SALT
WORLD OVER
Tupperware

so preppy!

serving suggestions

This is a hot take, but I've gotta come clean. I regret the day I started meal prepping our lunches.

It does make mornings in our house so much easier, and if I didn't make lunches ahead of time, Luis and I both would either not eat lunch (bad) or go out for lunch every day (even worse). So, the meal prepping is a necessary evil I must endure to ensure we don't overspend or go "hangry"—and I'm mostly talking about getting hangry myself here.

Let's be real. Cooking for a family is is a lot of work. We're just a couple, but sometimes the prep and planning can feel like a part-time job—and I don't even have kids! For all of y'all that do—bless you!

In our house, meal prepping typically consists of roasting a chicken (like the one on page 224), putting salad greens into containers, making the salad dressing on page 28, and chopping up any loose vegetables rolling around the crisper drawer. When I get a wild hair, I might candy some nuts to use as a salad topper, but most weeks I find something crunchy in the pantry—often the fried onions meant for topping green bean casserole—and call it a day.

I share all of this to show that behind all the fancy Instagram posts, pretty photo shoots, and fun work trips, I'm still going through the meal prep trenches. Being "so preppy" isn't as glamorous as it all seems, so here's to all of you doing your best to get your people fed. I'm proud of you.

RUSSBE

pineapple casserole (page 220)

lacy cornbread (opposite)

nana's marinated peas (page 212)

lacy cornbread

SERVES 10
ACTIVE: 35 MINUTES
TOTAL: 35 MINUTES

¾ cup (180 ml) canola oil

1 cup (138 g) self-rising, buttermilk-enriched white cornmeal mix, such as White Lily or Martha White

½ teaspoon kosher salt

¾ cup (180 ml) hot tap water

These crispy, golden rounds of cornbread go by many other names, like hoecakes, hot-water cornbread, lacy hoecakes, johnnycakes, and more. Although they taste great on their own, they're best served as an accompaniment to casseroles or side dishes. I like to spoon the perfect bite of green bean casserole, cornbread dressing, turkey, and cranberry sauce on a piece of lacy cornbread and eat it.

1. In a 10-inch (25-cm) nonstick skillet, heat oil to 375°F (190°C) over medium-high heat. Meanwhile, in a medium bowl, whisk together cornmeal mix, salt, and hot water. (Batter will be very thin.)

2. Carefully pour 2 tablespoons batter into hot oil. Batter will immediately spread out to about a 4-inch (10-cm) circle and appear lacy. Fry until golden on first side, 1 to 1½ minutes. Flip and fry until golden on second side, 1 to 1½ minutes. Place on a paper towel–lined plate to drain. Repeat procedure with remaining batter, stirring batter before each batch.

pineapple casserole

SERVES 8
ACTIVE: 15 MINUTES
TOTAL: 1 HOUR, 10 MINUTES

2 (20-ounce / 567-g) cans pineapple tidbits

¾ cup (150 g) granulated sugar

6 tablespoons (45 g) all-purpose flour

½ cup (120 ml) melted unsalted butter

¼ teaspoon kosher salt

1 block sharp Cheddar cheese (8 ounces / 225 g), shredded (2 cups), divided

1½ cups (135 g) buttery round cracker crumbs, such as Ritz

This recipe is one of my family's favorites, but I'm the first to admit it's definitely not for everyone. Upon first glance, the ingredients sound like they absolutely do not go together. If you're adventurous enough to give it a try, you might find, surprisingly, it somehow works. Pineapple casserole is very popular in my South Georgia neck of the woods, but there are other pockets of the South that serve up the bubbling cheesy casserole too. Where I'm from, it's commonly served alongside the savory sides at Thanksgiving and Easter, as it's a perfect pairing with ham and turkey. Of all the recipes in this book, I might be most excited if you told me you tried this one and discovered you love it.

1. Preheat oven to 300°F (150°C). Drain pineapple, reserving 6 tablespoons (90 ml) of the juice from the can. In a large bowl, whisk together reserved pineapple juice, sugar, flour, butter, and salt until smooth. Fold in pineapple tidbits and 1½ cups (170 g) of the Cheddar. Transfer mixture to an 11 by 7-inch (28 by 17-cm) baking dish and bake in preheated oven until cheese is starting to melt, about 25 minutes.

2. Remove baking dish from oven. Increase oven temperature to 350°F (175°C). Top pineapple mixture with remaining Cheddar and cracker crumbs. Return to oven and continue baking for 20 to 25 minutes, or until edges are bubbly and crackers are golden brown.

rebecca's brussels sprouts and bacon salad

SERVES 4 TO 6
ACTIVE: 25 MINUTES
TOTAL: 50 MINUTES

1 small garlic clove, peeled

2 anchovies, packed in oil

¼ cup (13 g) chopped fresh flat-leaf parsley

2 tablespoons chopped fresh chives

1 tablespoon chopped fresh tarragon

1 tablespoon fresh lemon juice, from 1 lemon

¼ cup (60 ml) whole buttermilk

⅓ cup (75 ml) mayonnaise

⅛ teaspoon freshly ground black pepper

5 slices bacon, cut into ½-inch (12-mm) pieces

1 sweet onion

1 pound (455 g) fresh Brussels sprouts

Every single day I get to work, I thank God for Rebecca Lang. Rebecca gave me my start years ago while I was a student at the University of Georgia. Because of her, I know fifty-one ways to fry a chicken, how to test and develop recipes, how to tackle a cookbook proposal and book map, how to pack and unpack a traveling kitchen for cooking demos on the road, and how to stick up for myself when no one else will. She started as my mentor and has become a very dear friend. During my time as her assistant, she wrote two books—one entirely devoted to fried chicken, and *The Southern Vegetable Book*, a complete one-eighty from all things fried. While I loved every single fried chicken recipe in that book, this Brussels sprouts salad is one that stays in my dinner and lunch rotation. My cookbook wouldn't be complete without a Rebecca recipe, because without her, I wouldn't have a book at all.

1. Pulse garlic and anchovies in a food processor until finely chopped. Add in parsley, chives, tarragon, lemon juice, buttermilk, mayonnaise, and black pepper; process until smooth. Set dressing aside while you make the salad, or transfer to an airtight container and refrigerate until ready to use, up to 2 days.

2. Cook bacon in a large skillet over medium-low heat, about 15 minutes, or until crispy. Using a slotted spoon, remove bacon, reserving drippings in skillet. Drain and set aside.

3. Cut onion in half. Slice halves into ¼-inch (6-mm) slices. Cook in hot drippings over medium-low heat for about 12 minutes, stirring often, until lightly browned.

4. While onion cooks, trim outer leaves and stems from Brussels sprouts; discard. Cut Brussels sprouts in half lengthwise; then cut into ¼-inch (6-mm) slices.

5. In a large bowl, toss together Brussels sprouts, onion, and desired amount of dressing. Sprinkle with bacon just before serving. Serve immediately.

ivy's take: If you have any remaining dressing, serve it with crudités, potato chips, or any grilled meat!

the southern summer vegetable plate

My idea of the perfect meal is a Southern-style summer vegetable plate. For me, the perfect one has a few crucial components: something creamy, something fresh, and something fried. Every summer, I set aside a weekend to take the time to make a proper veggie plate, and all three of these dishes will be on it. Every vegetable can be enjoyed on its own or all together on your fork to make the perfect bite. For a truly transformative experience, dip your fried okra into your creamed corn—the two together create magic.

butter-glazed field peas

SERVES 4
ACTIVE: 10 MINUTES
TOTAL: 10 MINUTES

½ cup (120 ml) chicken stock or broth

5 tablespoons (71 g) salted butter, divided

3 cups (555 g) cooked field peas or 2 (15-ounce / 425-g) cans field peas, drained

¾ teaspoon kosher salt

2 tablespoons chopped fresh chives

2 tablespoons chopped fresh dill

2 teaspoons chopped fresh thyme

1 tablespoon fresh lemon juice (from 1 lemon)

1. In a large nonstick skillet, heat chicken stock over medium-high heat until steaming. Add 4 tablespoons (55 g) butter to warmed chicken stock and cook, swirling the skillet often, until butter is melted, about 2 minutes. Continue cooking and swirling the skillet until mixture begins to bubble and mostly come together, about 1 more minute. Add peas to skillet and cook, stirring occasionally, until warmed through, about 2 minutes.

2. Add remaining 1 tablespoon butter to skillet along with salt, chives, dill, thyme, and lemon juice. Stir gently to incorporate, then remove from heat and let sit until butter just melts. Serve immediately.

smashed fried okra

SERVES 4
ACTIVE: 30 MINUTES
TOTAL: 30 MINUTES

Canola oil, for frying

½ pound (225 g) fresh okra

½ cup (120 ml) whole buttermilk

1½ cups (270 g) finely ground plain cornmeal

1½ teaspoons kosher salt, plus more to taste

1 In a 4 to 5-quart (3.8 to 4.7-L) Dutch oven, pour oil to a depth of 1 inch (2.5 cm) and heat oil to 350°F (175°C). While oil is heating, use a meat mallet or hammer to smash okra pods so that the pointed tips are frayed, but the stem end is still intact.

2 In a shallow medium bowl, place buttermilk with smashed okra and toss okra in buttermilk so the pods are evenly coated. In another shallow medium bowl, stir together cornmeal and salt, then dredge okra in cornmeal to coat. Be sure to shake any excess cornmeal off okra pods before carefully dropping okra into the hot oil. Fry okra in 3 batches until golden brown and crisp, turning occasionally to ensure even browning, 4 to 5 minutes per batch. Okra tends to pop when submerged in hot oil, so be careful and step back from the stove while frying. Be sure to allow oil to come back to temperature before frying next batch. Use a slotted spoon to transfer fried okra to a paper towel–lined plate to drain and season with more salt if desired. Serve immediately.

old-fashioned creamed corn

SERVES 4
ACTIVE: 1 HOUR
TOTAL: 1 HOUR

9 ears (3½ pounds / 1.6 kg) corn, any color

4 tablespoons (55 g) salted butter

¼ cup (60 ml) heavy cream

1¼ teaspoons kosher salt

1 tablespoon finely chopped fresh chives, for garnish

1 Cut kernels off corn cobs with a knife or a corn creamer into a medium bowl. If you don't have a corn creamer, run a spoon or butter knife along the corn cobs to scrape out any leftover kernel bits and all of the "milk" from the cob into bowl with kernels.

2 In a medium saucepan, melt butter over medium heat. Add kernels and any scraped milk and kernel bits to the melted butter and cook over medium-low heat, stirring occasionally, until slightly thickened and creamy, about 20 minutes.

3 Stir heavy cream into saucepan and cook over low heat, stirring occasionally, until very creamy and slightly reduced, 7 to 10 minutes. Remove from heat and stir in salt. Transfer creamed corn to a serving bowl and garnish with chives.

tip: If you do not have a corn creamer, the best way to cut the kernels off the cob is to use a Bundt pan. Place a Bundt pan on the counter, and place 1 cob into the center hole to hold the cob in place. Then, use a knife to carefully cut the kernels off of the cob; the Bundt pan will catch all of the kernels as they are cut.

if this isn't southern . . . Norpro makes old-fashioned corn cutters and creamers, which, as the name suggests, both cut the kernels and cream the milky juices from the cobs for the best creamed corn.

sunday roasted chicken

SERVES 4
ACTIVE: 20 MINUTES
TOTAL: 1 HOUR, 15 MINUTES

1 (4½-pound / 2-kg) whole chicken

3 tablespoons extra-virgin olive oil, divided

5 teaspoons House Seasoning (page 20)

1 teaspoon kosher salt

This is a really good, really easy roasted chicken recipe. I roast one almost every Sunday to use in different ways throughout the week, because if I've got some cooked chicken, I can turn almost anything into a meal.

1 Preheat oven to 425°F (220°C). Remove chicken from packaging and pat very dry with paper towels.

2 Drizzle a 10-inch (25-cm) cast-iron skillet with 2 tablespoons of the oil. Drizzle chicken evenly with remaining 1 tablespoon oil, being sure to rub oil on all sides of the chicken. Rub house seasoning evenly over all sides of chicken and into the cavity. Sprinkle salt evenly over all sides of chicken, then place chicken, breast-side up, in skillet. Tuck wing tips underneath.

3 Bake in preheated oven for 1 hour to 1 hour and 10 minutes, or until a thermometer inserted into the thickest portion of the chicken breasts registers 155°F (68°C). (I would start checking the temperature of your chicken at 50 to 55 minutes, as some ovens cook hotter than others, and your bird might not be exactly 4½ pounds / 2 kg.)

4 Use tongs to lift the chicken out of the skillet (this is easiest if you insert one tong into the cavity of the bird and use the other to grip the breasts on top) and onto a cutting board. (Be sure your board has ridges to catch any juices, or use a rimmed platter.) Let chicken rest 10 minutes before slicing.

tip: I highly recommend serving the chicken with a spoonful of the pan drippings for maximum flavor and juiciness.

ivy's take! I prefer to eat my leg quarters the day I roast the chicken and save the breast meat for easy meal prep during the week. This is totally optional—you can eat your whole bird the day you roast it, or use it all for meal prep!

Pasta Veloce
Simple
Atomic Habits
TIMELESS JOURNEYS
CORN
Southern

TEQUILA & TACOS
REBECCA LANG
MASTERING the ART of SOUTHERN COOKING
Dupree & Graubart
RECIPE REVIVAL
THIS BOOK
COOKBOOK
Rebecca Lang

fried catfish

SERVES 6
ACTIVE: 20 MINUTES
TOTAL: 1 HOUR, 20 MINUTES

2 pounds (910 kg) catfish fillets, cut into 2½-ounce (70-g) pieces

¼ cup (60 ml) whole buttermilk

1 tablespoon Old Bay seasoning

1 tablespoon Creole seasoning, such as Tony Chachere's

1 tablespoon all-purpose seasoning, such as WayneO's Southern Seasoning

¾ cup (100 g) plain enriched yellow cornmeal

¾ cup (180 g) finely ground white cornmeal

¼ cup (30 g) soft winter wheat self-rising flour, such as White Lily

½ teaspoon kosher salt

½ teaspoon freshly ground black pepper

Peanut oil, for frying

I know many people cooking from this book might be tempted to skip over this recipe. Honestly, I almost didn't include it for that reason. But when I tasted the fish hot out of the fryer, I knew it had to make the cut. If you find yourself anywhere near some good, small, freshly caught catfish (not the ginormous fillets from ten-pounders you find at most seafood stores), grab it and fry it up. When it's hot and crisp, not much can beat it.

1. In a shallow bowl, place catfish fillets with buttermilk; toss to coat. Let stand 5 minutes while you stir together seasonings.

2. In a small bowl, combine Old Bay, Creole seasoning, and all-purpose seasoning. Season fish evenly with 1½ tablespoons of the mixture; toss to coat well. Cover with plastic wrap and refrigerate at least 1 hour or up to 4 hours.

3. In a large Dutch oven or heavy-bottomed pot, pour oil to a depth of 3 inches (7.5 cm) and heat to 350°F (175°C) over medium-high heat. While oil is coming to temperature, whisk together plain and finely ground cornmeal, self-rising flour, salt, pepper, and remaining seasoning mixture in a large bowl. Dredge fillets in cornmeal mixture to coat well, shaking off excess before dropping fillets into hot oil. Fry fish in 3 batches for about 6 minutes per batch. Fish will be crisp, deep golden brown, and should float at top of oil when done. Transfer to a paper towel–lined plate. Allow oil to come back up to 350°F (175°C) before frying the next batch.

note: For crispy results, each fillet should be about 2½ ounces (70 g). Smaller fish work best; if large, cut to size. Most market fillets are 5 to 7 ounces (140 to 200 g), so cut into 2 or 3 pieces.

slow-cooker short ribs with pork rind gremolata

SERVES 4
ACTIVE: 35 MINUTES
TOTAL: 35 MINUTES, PLUS 7 HOURS SLOW-COOKING

3 pounds (1.4 kg) beef chuck (English-cut) short ribs (about eight 7-ounce / 200-g short ribs)

1 teaspoon freshly ground black pepper

2¾ teaspoons kosher salt, divided

2 tablespoons canola oil

4 cups (440 g) sliced yellow onions (from 2 medium onions)

1½ cups (360 ml) beef stock

½ cup (120 ml) fresh orange juice, plus 1 teaspoon grated orange zest

1 (2-inch / 5-cm) piece fresh ginger, unpeeled and sliced

1 garlic head, halved crosswise and loose, papery skins discarded

1 tablespoon cornstarch

1 tablespoon cold water

½ cup (40 g) crumbled pork rinds

2 tablespoons chopped fresh flat-leaf parsley

Hot cooked grits or polenta, for serving

During the holidays, my kitchen never closes. From family gatherings to cookie exchanges with friends, I host and attend more parties than at any other time of the year. Like most people, I have my tried-and-true favorites that always make a comeback. Some are intensive baking projects, like intricate iced cookies or fancy cakes, and others are quick, crowd-pleasing dishes that I can throw together at a moment's notice.

This recipe checks every box for a dinner party menu. It's a fresh take on a comforting classic that looks impressive without being too fussy. And best of all, it's mostly made in a slow cooker, which gives me plenty of time to mingle instead of standing over the stove. This can even be made a day or two in advance. Even though good food is always at the center of every Southern celebration, it's getting to spend extra time with the ones we love that matters most.

1 Sprinkle ribs evenly with pepper and 2 teaspoons of the salt. In a 12-inch (30.5 cm) cast-iron skillet, heat oil over high heat. When oil is very hot, add ribs to skillet, working in batches if needed. Cook until well browned on all sides, about 10 minutes. Transfer ribs, bone sides up, to a 5- or 6-quart (4.7- or 5.7-L) slow cooker.

2 Reduce heat under skillet to medium-high. Add onions and ½ teaspoon of the salt to skillet and cook, stirring often, until softened, about 8 minutes. Using a slotted spoon, transfer onions to slow cooker; discard drippings in skillet. Add beef stock, orange juice, ginger, and garlic to slow cooker. Cover and cook on low until meat is very tender and falling off the bones, about 7 hours.

3 Remove ribs from slow cooker and set aside. Pour remaining mixture in slow cooker through a fine mesh strainer into a medium saucepan; discard solids. Cook liquid in pan over medium-high heat until reduced by half (about 1 cup / 240 ml), 10 to 12 minutes. In a small bowl, stir together cornstarch and cold water; whisk into liquid in pan and cook until sauce simmers, 2 to 3 minutes. Remove from heat.

4 In a small bowl, stir together pork rinds, parsley, orange zest, and remaining ¼ teaspoon salt. Spoon sauce over grits or polenta on a plate and place ribs on sauce. Garnish with pork rind mixture and serve.

BAMA FOOD PRODUCTS BORDEN INC.
BAMA
BORDEN
ALABAMA 35217
REFRIGERATE AFTER OPENING

aunt bean's mayo jar cucumbers

MAKES ABOUT 2 CUPS (480 ML)
ACTIVE: 15 MINUTES
TOTAL: 4 HOURS, 15 MINUTES

⅓ cup (75 ml) mayonnaise

1½ tablespoons distilled white vinegar

4 teaspoons granulated sugar

¼ teaspoon kosher salt

1¾ cups (200 g) thinly sliced English cucumber (from 1 cucumber)

1 cup (110 g) thinly sliced sweet onion (from 1 small onion)

Freshly ground black pepper, for serving

Fresh dill, for serving

Many of my family's prized recipes come from my Aunt Bean. She was a fantastic cook, known for singing hymns in the kitchen while she cooked. She had a successful career, starting as a secretary and ending as the vice president of Moultrie Federal Savings Bank, and she helped her husband run their Angus farm. She played piano and was the treasurer for the church her daddy built, but she loved drinking coffee from a mug that read, "I love Jesus, but I cuss a little." Barely over five feet tall, what she lacked in height she made up for in personality. She lit up every room she entered. When I think of all the strong women in my family who've inspired and encouraged me to where I am today, Aunt Bean is near the top. Every time I reach the end of a mayonnaise jar, which in my line of work is more often than most, I think of her and her knack for making even the smallest things more wonderful.

When you've got about ⅓ cup (75 ml) of mayonnaise left in a 30-ounce (887-ml) jar, add vinegar, sugar, and salt to the jar and shake well to combine. Layer in your sliced cucumbers and onions, alternating each as you fill the jar. Once your jar is full of veggies, shake well to combine. Place in the refrigerator at least 4 hours before serving, or up to 2 weeks. Add more cucumbers and onions as your jar starts to run low, if desired. Serve garnished with black pepper and fresh dill.

One of the things I'm most thankful for about my childhood is that we lived in the same town as my mama's parents. They came to every piano recital, choir performance, award ceremony, and even the few sports I reluctantly tried. (I quickly learned that sports were not my strong suit, and I should stick to more artsy endeavors.) I went out to eat with Papa on Tuesday nights and played bingo with Nana at the country club on Thursdays. So many of my happiest moments involved the two of them.

Perhaps some of my most favorite memories are the ones at their house. I spent many Friday nights over at Nana and Papa's. I can remember waking up to the smell of bacon frying and grits bubbling on the stove. Every time I make bacon in my own house now, which has original heart pine flooring like Nana and Papa's house did, something about the smell of bacon and old house takes me back to Saturday mornings on Faison Road. The golf channel would always be playing in the background; the soft claps were the soundtrack to our slow Saturdays. We'd play out in the yard or in the playhouse Papa had built just for his three grandchildren, while Nana made a lunch of pimiento cheese, salad, fried chicken, and sliced tomatoes. In the afternoons, we crowded around the breakfast table to make tea cakes, or we made potholders on antique red metal looms. Nana taught me to cross-stitch and tat lace. Papa taught me how to hit a golf ball and drive a lawn mower. So much of who I am today is because of afternoons at Nana and Papa's.

My papa passed away a few years ago, and there isn't a day that goes by that I don't miss him. I'm lucky enough to get to see Nana every time I go home to Moultrie, and even luckier that she (reluctantly) agreed to come to Birmingham to cook with me in my own kitchen for a photo shoot. We made two of my favorites from her recipe collection, fried pies and tea cakes, which you can find on the next pages. While she loves to cook, it took a few glass bottle Coca-Colas to convince her to smile for the camera. I'll forever be thankful for the chance to capture these memories in this book. She might not admit it, but she had (almost) as much fun as we used to on our treasured Saturday afternoons.

nana's fried pies
(page 237)

nana's tea cakes
(page 236)

nana's tea cakes

MAKES ABOUT 4 DOZEN TEA CAKES
ACTIVE: 20 MINUTES
TOTAL: 50 MINUTES

- 3½ cups (440 g) all-purpose flour
- 1 cup (200 g) granulated sugar
- 2 teaspoons baking powder
- 1 teaspoon kosher salt
- 1 cup (225 g) salted butter, cut into ½-inch (12-mm) pieces, at room temperature
- 2 large eggs, lightly beaten
- 1 tablespoon vanilla extract

What I love most about Nana's tea cakes and her fried pies in particular is that one could take up a good chunk of a Saturday afternoon, and the other is a quick and easy way to keep little hands busy. Depending on the situation, Nana was always ready with one or the other. Both bring back sweet memories I'll cherish forever.

1. Preheat oven to 400°F (205°C). Line two baking sheets with parchment paper. In a large bowl, whisk together flour, sugar, baking powder, and salt. Add butter pieces to bowl and mix with hands, pinching butter into flour mixture with your fingers until mixture resembles chunky wet sand. Add eggs and vanilla into flour mixture and mix well with hands until dough comes together into a smooth ball.

2. Roll dough, about 1 tablespoon at a time, into gumball-size balls and place on prepared baking sheets about 1 inch (2.5 cm) apart. Bake in preheated oven 7 to 9 minutes, or until lightly golden brown and set, rotating baking sheets halfway through. Let cool completely on wire racks, about 20 minutes.

behind the scenes I developed this recipe using Nana's handwritten recipe card as a guide. I followed it exactly—or as exactly as I could. She gives two different instructions for making these tea cakes. One calls for rolling the dough into balls "about the size of a gumball" and placing them on a baking sheet. She also says you can roll the dough and use a small round cutter to make the tea cakes, too. These two methods give very different results. One is thinner and more wafer-like. The other is thicker and chewier. Growing up, we always rolled and cut our tea cakes when we made them with Nana. The thinner ones always got a little too crisp for my liking, so when I tried the gumball method, I much preferred the chewier cookie. So, that's what I called for doing in the recipe here. Well, when it came time for the photo shoot with my Nana (see page 235), I started making the tea cakes my way. She immediately took over and said the thinner, rolling pin method was better. If you look at the photos, you can see us each doing them our own way. We had everyone on set try them, and it was pretty divided on which style of tea cake people liked best. According to Nana, my version isn't a true tea cake, but it does taste good. Since we couldn't agree, I'll let y'all decide which you like best.

nana's fried pies

SERVES 8
ACTIVE: 30 MINUTES
TOTAL: 30 MINUTES

1 (21-ounce / 595-g) can apple or peach pie filling

8 super soft (6-inch / 15-cm) flour tortillas, such as Mission

¼ cup (60 ml) canola oil

1 tablespoon granulated sugar

Nana loved cooking, but she was never above a shortcut that got her out of the kitchen faster. Her fried pies use flour tortillas in place of dough, and they can be made in no time.

1. If the fruit in your pie filling is in whole slices, place pie filling in a food processor or blender and pulse until finely chopped, about 6 pulses. (You don't want large chunks of sliced fruit for these pies.)

2. Fill a small bowl with water and set it by your workstation. Spoon about 3 tablespoons filling onto one tortilla, being sure to only spread the filling over half of the tortilla. Wet your fingertip in the water and run it around the entire edge of the tortilla, continuing to get more water to dampen the tortilla edge. Fold the unfilled tortilla side over the filled side to create a half circle, then use a fork to crimp the edges tightly, but try not to press so hard you poke a hole in the tortilla. Continue with remaining pie filling and tortillas.

3. In a 10-inch (25-cm) cast-iron skillet, heat oil over medium heat. When oil reaches 350°F (175°C), place two pies in hot oil and fry until golden brown and crisp on first side, about 1 minute. Flip, then continue cooking second side until golden and crisp, about 1 minute more. Remove pies from oil and let drain on paper towels while you continue frying remaining pies.

4. When all pies are fried, sprinkle sugar evenly over both sides of each pie. Serve warm.

strudel with fried apples

SERVES 8
ACTIVE: 30 MINUTES
TOTAL: 1 HOUR, 10 MINUTES

2 pounds (6 cups / 910 g) Honeycrisp apples, peeled and sliced into ¼-inch (6-mm) slices (about 4 medium apples)

¼ cup (55 g) packed light brown sugar

1 tablespoon bacon drippings

½ teaspoon ground cinnamon

¼ teaspoon kosher salt

1 teaspoon all-purpose flour, plus more for work surface

½ (17.3-ounce / 490-g) package frozen puff pastry, such as Pepperidge Farm, thawed

1 large egg

1 teaspoon water

1 tablespoon granulated sugar

Vanilla ice cream (optional)

During my ninth-grade choir trip to Austria, I swooned over a Sacher torte, savored my first real schnitzel, and realized the frozen toaster pastries were, in fact, not how strudels were supposed to taste. Surrounded by scenery straight out of *The Sound of Music*, each bite had me singing about girls in white dresses with blue satin sashes. Though I'd never admit it to an Austrian, I remember thinking then that the flaky pastry would be even more divine if it were filled with the Southern-style fried apples made famous by a popular US-interstate country store. When I'm in need of an easy-yet-impressive fall dessert, I simply remember my favorite things—and whip up this crisp (fried) apple strudel.

1. In a large skillet, cook apples, brown sugar, bacon drippings, cinnamon, and salt over medium heat, stirring occasionally, until liquid has evaporated and apples soften, about 12 minutes. Add flour to mixture and toss to coat. Cook, stirring occasionally, for 1 minute. Remove from heat; let cool 20 minutes.

2. Meanwhile, preheat oven to 400°F (205°C). Line a large rimmed baking sheet with parchment paper; set aside.

3. Roll thawed puff pastry sheet into a 14 by 9-inch (35.5 by 23-cm) rectangle on a lightly floured work surface. Transfer pastry sheet to prepared baking sheet. In a small bowl, whisk together egg and water; set aside.

4. Using scissors and starting at one long edge of pastry sheet, cut 1-inch-wide (2.5-cm) slits running from pastry edge toward pastry center, with each slit 2½ inches (6 cm) long. You will end up with 14 strips cut along that long edge. Repeat process on other long edge of pastry sheet. Spoon the cooled apple mixture evenly down the length of the pastry center, avoiding the cuts' edges on both sides. Brush some of the egg-water mixture lightly over cut strips. Starting with the top left strip, fold the strip over the apples in the center of the pastry at a slight angle. Fold the top right strip over apples at a slight angle to meet the far edge of left strip in center. Repeat with remaining strips, going from left to right to create a braided herringbone effect down center of pastry. Brush strudel with remaining egg-water mixture and sprinkle with granulated sugar.

5. Bake in preheated oven until pastry is crisp and golden, 15 to 18 minutes. Let cool 5 minutes on baking sheet. Slice evenly into 8 portions. Serve with vanilla ice cream, if desired.

apples foster

SERVES 4
ACTIVE: 20 MINUTES
TOTAL: 20 MINUTES

6 tablespoons (85 g) salted butter

2 pounds (8 cups / 910 g) Honeycrisp apples, unpeeled, cored, and cut into ¾- to 1-inch-thick (2- to 2.5-cm) wedges (about 4 medium apples)

¾ cup (165 g) packed light brown sugar

¼ teaspoon ground cinnamon

¼ teaspoon kosher salt

½ cup (4 ounces / 120 ml) bourbon

1 cup (32 g) Easy Granola (page 114)

Vanilla ice cream

In the South, when the weather starts to cool and the leaves begin to turn, many people start itching to pull out their pie plates and rolling pins. The bucket list of fall baking projects seems endless: apple pie, pumpkin bread, pecan pie, bread pudding (is that seasonal?). But for me, fall is one of the busiest times of year. I'm doing well if dinner ends up on my table—let alone dessert! But there are some nights when a hankering for a fall dessert just can't be ignored, in which case I pull out a skillet and make apples foster. It takes about 20 minutes from start to finish (if you keep granola on hand like I do), and it satisfies everything I could ever want from a dessert. Sweet, crunchy, hot, cold, and utterly decadent—it will have you rethinking any fall baking project that requires a rolling pin ever again.

1. In a large nonstick skillet, melt butter over medium heat until bubbly. Add apples and cook, stirring occasionally, until apples are browned and slightly softened, about 5 minutes. Stir in brown sugar, cinnamon, and salt until combined. Cook over medium heat, stirring often, until sugar dissolves, apples are tender, and brown sugar mixture is slightly thickened, 6 to 8 minutes.

2. Carefully add bourbon to skillet and cook over medium heat, stirring often, until alcohol aroma dissipates, 2 to 3 minutes. (If using a gas cooktop, mixture in skillet may light on fire because of high alcohol content. Use caution, and let cook until flame is out.)

3. Using a slotted spoon, distribute apples evenly among four serving bowls. Reserve ¼ cup (60 ml) sauce; divide remaining sauce evenly among bowls. Top each bowl with ¼ cup (8 g) granola and a scoop of ice cream. Drizzle evenly with reserved sauce. Serve immediately.

strawberry shortcake sheet cake

SERVES 12
ACTIVE: 30 MINUTES
TOTAL: 2 HOURS, 10 MINUTES

2 pounds (910 g) fresh strawberries

Cooking spray

2¼ cups (180 g) soft winter wheat self-rising flour, such as White Lily

1 cup (125 g) all-purpose flour, plus more for dusting

½ teaspoon kosher salt

¾ cup (150 g) granulated sugar, divided

¼ cup (55 g) cold unsalted butter, cut into ¼-inch (6-mm) cubes

1 cup (240 ml) whole buttermilk

2 teaspoons grated lemon zest (from 1 lemon)

1⅔ cups (405 ml) heavy whipping cream, divided

3 teaspoons vanilla extract, divided

1¼ tablespoons unsalted butter, melted

2 tablespoons sanding sugar

1 (8-ounce / 226-g) container mascarpone

¼ cup (30 g) powdered sugar

Growing up, our version of "strawberry shortcake" was an angel food cake trifle layered with whipped cream and strawberries. It was my papa's favorite dessert. It wasn't until I started cooking professionally that I learned strawberry shortcake doesn't actually involve angel food cake at all. The real strawberry shortcake is basically a glorified biscuit, sweetened and served with fruit and cream. My version is oversized and studded with strawberries throughout, reminiscent of the trifle of my childhood. To me, it's the best of both worlds, and one I know Papa would love.

1 Hull 1 pound (455 g) of the fresh strawberries and cut in half lengthwise; set aside. Hull and chop strawberries from remaining 1 pound (455 g) berries to measure 1 cup (165 g); set aside. (Reserve remaining whole berries for another use.)

2 Preheat oven to 400°F (205°C). Coat a 13 by 9-inch (33 by 23-cm) rimmed baking sheet with cooking spray. In a large bowl, whisk together self-rising flour, all-purpose flour, salt, and ½ cup (100 g) of the granulated sugar. Cut cold butter cubes into flour mixture until butter pieces are evenly coated and pea size. Gently fold in buttermilk, lemon zest, ⅔ cup (165 ml) of the whipping cream, and 1 teaspoon of the vanilla until mixture just comes together but is still lumpy. Gently fold in reserved chopped strawberries.

3 Using a ¼-cup (60 ml) measuring cup dusted with all-purpose flour to prevent sticking, scoop slightly rounded dough mounds onto prepared baking sheet in 3 rows of 6 side-by-side mounds, continuing to flour measuring cup after each mound to prevent sticking. Brush dough mounds evenly with melted butter and sprinkle with sanding sugar.

4 Bake in preheated oven until golden brown, 28 to 32 minutes. Transfer baking sheet with shortcake to a wire rack and cool for 10 minutes. Transfer shortcake to wire rack; cool completely, about 1 hour.

5 Meanwhile, in a medium bowl, stir together halved strawberries and remaining ¼ cup (50 g) granulated sugar, and let stand until berries start to release their juices, 10 to 15 minutes. Gently stir together mascarpone, powdered sugar, and remaining 2 teaspoons vanilla in a

separate medium bowl until just combined. In a separate large bowl, pour remaining 1 cup (240 ml) whipping cream and beat with an electric mixer fitted with a whisk attachment on high speed until stiff peaks form, 2 to 3 minutes. Gently fold whipped cream into mascarpone mixture until just combined.

6 Spread whipped cream–mascarpone mixture over top of cooled shortcake, leaving edges exposed. Top with strawberry mixture and any accumulated juices. Slice evenly into 12 pieces and serve immediately.

When people ask me how my current job at *Southern Living* came to be, this is the story I tell them.

I started as a fellow in the *Southern Living* Test Kitchen in September 2016. I tested and developed recipes, helped stock and clean the food studio pantry and walk-ins, did the grocery shopping for the more senior recipe tester/developers, and assisted food stylists on photo shoots. One day after I finished grocery shopping, I didn't have any recipes to test or develop on my schedule. My manager told me I could make anything I wanted and maybe one of the brands would take the recipe and use it on their website. I knew immediately what I would make.

Where I'm from in South Georgia, little layer cakes are everywhere. Chocolate is the most common (and my favorite) flavor, but you can find them in caramel and lemon, too. The multilayered cakes were always at cake auctions, church picnics, baby showers, funerals, or even sliced and served on Styrofoam plates wrapped in plastic as a dessert option at barbecue joints and meat-and-threes. Little layer cakes were everywhere in my childhood, and it never occurred to me that they might not be a thing outside South Georgia.

I knew I needed to get the recipe just right. This cake takes lots of patience, a virtue that doesn't come to me naturally. I had a recipe for cooked chocolate icing written down by my nana as told to her by her mother, my great-grandmother, Granny. Granny's little layer cakes were known all over town. My mama got one every year for her birthday. Granny would always make twelve-layer cakes, until Mama turned thirteen, when she started adding a layer for each year until she turned eighteen. Mama remembers Granny making the layers like pancakes in a flat cast-iron skillet, but no one could remember her cake batter recipe. I wanted so desperately to figure it out.

I started gathering ingredients, turning on ovens, and prepping my pans. I did a little research to see if I could find some other little layer cake recipes out there but wasn't shocked when very little turned up. I decided to go with a thicker batter, spread thinly into parchment-lined cake pans and baked in a hot oven for a short amount of time. Granny's pancake method had never worked for me in the past, so this felt more realistic. While the icing boiled on the stove, I started assembling the cake, running from oven to oven every few minutes to grab a hot layer to add to the stack. Unlike other cake recipes out there, you add the icing while the layers are still warm. It was quite a sight to behold in the test kitchens. Word traveled throughout the building that the fellow was upstairs running from oven to oven attempting to make an eighteen-layer cake. People came from every floor to watch as I flipped hot cake layers on top of a thin layer of chocolate icing, then spread another thin layer on top. As I worked, I told the story about my granny's cakes and my mama's birthdays and how I was shocked that no one "in the *Southern Living* Test Kitchen of all places" had ever seen one of these cakes. To me, this cake was the epitome of Southern cakes. There are similar cakes out there, Maryland Smith Island cake and Louisiana Doberge cake, but this particular version really can only be found in pockets of South Georgia and South Alabama.

Two of the people that came to watch me bake were *Southern Living* editor in chief, Sid Evans, and director of video, Mike Grady. For the lowly test kitchen fellow, this was a huge deal. Both of them were so intrigued by my cake and its story, they asked me to make a video about it. I was hesitant. I started working in the test kitchens because I wanted to write recipes, and maybe one day write a cookbook, and teach cooking classes. Plus, this was a time before social media videos really started to become popular. I agreed to give it a go on the basis that if it turned out badly, they wouldn't post it—ha!

The approximately three-minute video was published in February 2017, and it was a mini–cooking show of sorts, much like what we all watch on social media these days. We didn't think it would gain much traction, but by the end of the summer, it was a viral success. *Southern Living* asked me to continue making videos for them, and I reluctantly agreed. Eighteen baking videos turned into thirty-six, which evolved into the launch of the *Hey Y'all* video series. That social media series turned into the *Southern Living Show*, which aired on nationally syndicated television networks. From there, I started writing a bimonthly column for *Southern Living* magazine, and now, exactly nine years after I started working as a fellow, I'm the author of this cookbook. All because one day, I made this cake.

little layer chocolate cake

SERVES 12
ACTIVE: 1 HOUR, 30 MINUTES
TOTAL: 2 HOURS

Cooking spray

9 (8-inch / 20-cm) round disposable aluminum pans

18 (8-inch / 20-cm) rounds parchment paper

24 ounces (720 ml) evaporated milk

6 cups (1.2 kg) granulated sugar, divided

1 cup (95 g) unsweetened cocoa powder

3 tablespoons light corn syrup

1 teaspoon kosher salt, divided

2½ cups (565 g) unsalted butter, softened, divided

6 large eggs

3 teaspoons vanilla extract, divided

4½ cups soft winter wheat all-purpose flour, such as White Lily

2 tablespoons baking powder

2 cups (480 ml) whole milk

This cake is a labor of love. Most people (even me) don't get it right on the first couple of tries. If yours comes out with more than ten layers, I'd call it a success. My favorite part about this cake is that on the outside it probably won't win any beauty contests, so you don't have to worry too much about how it looks. It's the inside that's the real showstopper.

1. Preheat oven to 425°F (220°C). Lightly grease disposable aluminum pans with cooking spray. Line the bottom of each pan with parchment paper, then spray the parchment paper with cooking spray. (You will end up using each of these 9 pans twice to make a total of 18 layers.)

2. To prepare icing, in a large saucepan, whisk together evaporated milk, 3 cups (600 g) sugar, cocoa powder, corn syrup, and ¼ teaspoon salt over medium heat. Attach a candy thermometer to pot and cook, whisking occasionally, to just at soft-ball stage (234 to 236°F / 112 to 113°C), about 15 minutes.

3. Meanwhile, in the bowl of a large heavy-duty stand mixer (or a large mixing bowl, if you have a handheld electric mixer), cream 1½ cups (3 sticks / 340 g) butter and remaining 3 cups (600 g) sugar.

4. Add in eggs, 2 at a time, until well incorporated, about 2 minutes. Add in 2 teaspoons vanilla.

5. In a medium bowl, sift together flour and baking powder. Add remaining ¾ teaspoon salt to sifted flour mixture.

6. Add flour mixture and milk to mixer bowl alternately in 3 additions, beginning and ending with flour mixture. Scrape down sides of mixer bowl with a rubber spatula and mix to incorporate fully, about 1 minute.

7. Once chocolate icing reaches soft-ball stage, reduce heat to simmer and add remaining 1 cup (2 sticks / 225 g) butter and remaining 1 teaspoon vanilla. Stir to melt butter, about 2 minutes. Maintain a very low simmer until first round of cake layers are out of oven.

8. Using a kitchen scale, add 4 ounces (115 g) of the batter to each prepared pan. Using an offset spatula, spread batter as evenly as possible on bottom of pans.

continued

9. Bake 3 or 4 layers at a time for 5 minutes in preheated oven. Remove from pan by placing a wire rack on top of pan and inverting pan to release cake layer. Remove parchment from cake layer and place first layer on cake stand. Remove icing from heat.

10. To assemble cake, pour about ¼ cup (60 ml) hot icing onto first cake layer, just enough to make a very thin layer of icing, but not enough to seep over sides of layer. Repeat with remaining baked layers as layers finish baking.

11. Prepare same cake pans again with more cooking spray and rounds of parchment; weigh out 4 ounces (115 g) of batter for each pan and spread layers as before. Bake 3 or 4 layers at a time for 5 minutes in preheated oven; continue layering cake with icing and baked cake layers. (If you find you are beginning to run out of icing, go ahead and use remaining icing to cover the outside of the cake as described in step 12. Depending on the weather, your candy thermometer, and a number of other uncontrollable factors, you might not end up with the same amount of icing each time.)

12. For top layer of icing, pour enough icing over top to seep over sides of cake. Use an offset spatula or small rubber spatula to spread a generous layer of icing to fully cover sides and top of cake. (Icing will be thicker at this point, and you will have some left over).

13. Let cake set at room temperature at least 30 minutes or up to 1 day before slicing.

lemon-cheese layer cake

SERVES 12
ACTIVE: 1 HOUR 20 MINUTES
TOTAL: 6 HOURS, 40 MINUTES

CAKE LAYERS:

Cooking spray

1 cup (225 g) unsalted butter, softened

2 cups (400 g) granulated sugar

6 egg whites

1½ teaspoons vanilla extract

1 teaspoon grated lemon zest (from 1 lemon)

3⅓ cups (435 g) bleached cake flour, such as Swans Down

1 tablespoon baking powder

¼ teaspoon kosher salt

1 cup (240 ml) whole milk

Lemon Curd (page 34)

LEMON BUTTERCREAM:

1 cup (225 g) unsalted butter, softened

3½ cups (440 g) powdered sugar

1 teaspoon grated lemon zest (from 1 lemon)

1 teaspoon vanilla extract

⅓ cup (75 ml) heavy whipping cream

Little layer cakes are becoming a lost art in the South (read more about their history on page 244). My lemon-cheese layer cake (one of the famed little layer cakes and properly pronounced with no pause between "lemon" and "cheese") is not like a cheesecake, as the name might suggest. The perfect balance of lemon curd filling and cake is what gives it that creamy consistency. My updated version is frosted with buttercream (unlike traditional recipes iced with lemon curd), which balances the tang and makes it more beautiful. It takes some effort, but once you slice into it, you'll know why these desserts have stood the test of time.

1. For the cake layers: Preheat oven to 375°F (190°C) with racks in middle and lower third positions. Coat four (8-inch / 20-cm) round cake pans with cooking spray and line with parchment paper; set aside. Beat butter in the bowl of a stand mixer fitted with a paddle attachment on medium speed until creamy, about 1 minute. Gradually add granulated sugar, beating until light and fluffy, 3 to 4 minutes. Stop mixer; scrape down sides. With mixer running on low speed, add egg whites, 1 at a time, stopping to scrape down sides as needed. Add vanilla and lemon zest; beat until just combined, about 30 seconds.

2. In a medium bowl, whisk together cake flour, baking powder, and salt. Add to butter mixture alternately with milk, beginning and ending with flour mixture, beating on low speed until just combined after each addition. Spread about ⅔ cup (165 ml) of batter into each of the prepared pans.

3. Bake cakes in preheated oven until a wooden pick inserted in center of cakes comes out clean, about 12 minutes. Cool in pans on wire racks for 5 minutes. Remove cakes from pans; place directly on wire racks to cool completely, about 30 minutes. Meanwhile, coat pans again with cooking spray and line again with parchment. Divide remaining batter evenly among pans (about ⅔ cup / 165 ml of batter per pan). Bake cakes per previous instructions. (Cake layers can be chilled overnight; tightly wrap each layer with plastic wrap.)

continued

4 **For the lemon buttercream:** In a large bowl, beat butter with an electric mixer on medium speed until creamy, about 1 minute. Gradually add powdered sugar, beating on low speed until combined, about 1 minute. Add lemon zest and vanilla, beating until just combined, about 10 seconds. With mixer running on medium speed, gradually add cream, beating until fluffy and spreadable, about 30 seconds.

5 Place one cake layer on a serving platter or a cake stand. Spoon ¼ cup (60 ml) lemon curd onto cake; spread evenly to edges using an offset spatula. Repeat process with six more cake layers and lemon curd. Top with remaining cake layer. (You should have about 1¼ cups / 300 ml filling remaining. Place in a piping bag or zip-top plastic bag; chill until ready to use.) Chill cake, uncovered, for 1 hour.

6 Spread lemon buttercream over top and sides of cake. Snip a ½-inch (12-mm) tip off piping bag. Pipe dots of reserved lemon curd filling, about the size of a quarter, around the top of the cake to create a ring, leaving about a 1-inch (2.5-cm) border around edge. Using an offset spatula, drag dots of filling toward center of cake to create a flowerlike pattern.

luis's favorite almond cake

SERVES 12
ACTIVE: 1 HOUR
TOTAL: 2 HOURS, 30 MINUTES

CAKE:

Cooking spray

½ cup (115 g) unsalted butter, at room temperature

2 cups (400 g) granulated sugar

½ cup (120 ml) vegetable oil

4 large eggs

2 teaspoons vanilla extract

1½ teaspoons almond extract

3½ cups (440 g) all-purpose flour

1 tablespoon baking powder

¾ teaspoon kosher salt

1 cup (240 ml) whole milk

BUTTERCREAM FROSTING:

1½ cups (340 g) unsalted butter, at room temperature

¾ teaspoon kosher salt

2 teaspoons vanilla extract

¾ teaspoon almond extract

4½ cups (450 g) powdered sugar, sifted

2 tablespoons whole milk

Sprinkles, optional

My husband, Luis, and I started dating a few weeks shy of his thirtieth birthday. As a way to woo him, I baked him this birthday cake. He loves the almond flavor of classic wedding cake and ANYTHING with sprinkles, so I'm pretty sure this cake is what sealed the deal. (I'm only partly kidding.) When you substitute vanilla for almond extract, this is a really good vanilla cake that can be frosted with any of your favorite frostings. To make it Luis-style, add some sprinkles to the batter before baking for a fun confetti cake surprise.

1. **Prepare the cake layers:** Preheat oven to 325°F (165°C). Lightly grease three (8-inch / 20-cm) round cake pans with cooking spray. Line the bottom of each pan with parchment, then spray the parchment with cooking spray.

2. In the bowl of a heavy-duty stand mixer (or a large mixing bowl, if you have a handheld electric mixer), beat butter and sugar on high speed until almost light and fluffy, about 3 minutes. Add oil to bowl and mix on medium-high speed until light and fluffy, about 2 minutes more. Add eggs to mixer bowl one at a time and mix on medium speed until just incorporated after each addition, stopping to scrape down the sides of the bowl as needed. Beat in vanilla and almond extracts.

3. In a large bowl, stir together flour, baking powder, and salt. Add flour mixture to mixer bowl alternately with milk, beating on medium-low speed until just combined after each addition, starting and ending with flour mixture. Divide batter evenly among three prepared pans, spreading into an even layer. Bake in preheated oven until a toothpick inserted in the center comes out clean, 30 to 32 minutes, rotating pans halfway through baking time.

4. Remove pans from oven and let cool in pans on wire racks for 10 minutes, then flip cakes onto wire racks to cool completely, about 1 hour. Frost immediately, or wrap each layer individually in plastic wrap, then freeze until ready to frost. Let thaw almost completely before frosting. (A chilled cake will frost much easier than a room temperature one, but allow the frozen cakes to thaw slightly before frosting.)

continued

5 **Prepare the buttercream:** In a large mixing bowl or the bowl of a stand mixer, beat butter on medium speed until smooth, about 1 minute. Beat in salt, and vanilla and almond extracts. Gradually add powdered sugar, beating well after each addition, scraping down the sides of the bowl as needed. Add milk and beat on medium speed until very smooth, about 1 minute. Use immediately, or store in an airtight container in the refrigerator for up to 3 days. To use chilled frosting, let sit at room temperature 30 minutes, then beat with an electric mixer to smooth before using.

6 **Frost the cake:** Spread about 2 teaspoons frosting onto a cake stand. This will help your bottom layer stay in place while you frost your cake. Place first cake layer onto cake stand, top side up, and top with about ¾ cup (168 g) of the frosting. Spread into an even layer with an offset spatula. Place second cake layer, top side up, on top of first, then top with another ¾ cup (168 g) of frosting and spread in an even layer. Place third cake layer, top side down, on top, then frost entire cake with remaining frosting and an offset spatula. Garnish with more sprinkles, if desired.

king cake beignets

MAKES 3 DOZEN
ACTIVE: 50 MINUTES
TOTAL: 4 HOURS, 50 MINUTES, INCLUDING CHILLING

1 teaspoon active dry yeast (from one ¼-ounce / 7-g envelope)

¾ cup (180 ml) warm water (105 to 115°F / 41 to 46°C), divided

4 tablespoons (50 g) granulated sugar, divided

1 large egg, lightly beaten

½ cup (120 ml) evaporated milk

¾ teaspoon kosher salt, divided

2 tablespoons vegetable shortening

¾ teaspoon ground cinnamon

3½ cups (475 g) bread flour, divided, plus more for work surface

Cooking spray

3 tablespoons (1½ ounces / 40 g) cream cheese, at room temperature

½ tablespoon unsalted butter, melted

½ tablespoon whole milk

½ teaspoon vanilla extract

6 tablespoons (12 g) powdered sugar, sifted

Vegetable oil, for frying

Green, purple, and yellow sanding sugars

When I was growing up in Georgia, we didn't pay much attention to Fat Tuesday. I'd heard of the parades, but the celebratory day seemed reserved for those fun-loving crowds in New Orleans or South Alabama. That all changed when I was a teenager visiting family in the small town of Lizana, Mississippi, near the coast. It was my first Carnival, and we were greeted by massive tables mounded with crawfish. That night, I tasted the lip-puckering heat of a crawfish boil and then found the baby in my first slice of king cake. (Tradition says if you find the little plastic baby figurine hidden in a king cake, you're in charge of providing king cake for the next party.)

Every year since, I've celebrated Fat Tuesday like it's my first one all over again. I don't always get around to the boil, but I do make sure some form of king cake is on the menu. One year, I combined two of my favorite Mardi Gras desserts to create these king cake beignets. The pillowy-soft treats are drizzled in a cream cheese glaze and sprinkled with crunchy sanding sugars in purple, green, and gold. The best part? You can make the dough ahead so you'll have more time to let the good times roll.

1. In the bowl of a stand mixer fitted with a dough hook attachment, stir together yeast, ¼ cup (60 ml) of the warm water, and ½ teaspoon of the granulated sugar. Let stand until foamy, about 5 minutes. Stir in egg, evaporated milk, ½ teaspoon of the salt, and remaining 3 tablespoons plus 2½ teaspoons granulated sugar.

2. In a medium bowl, stir together shortening and remaining ½ cup (120 ml) warm water until melted. Add this to yeast mixture. Beat on low speed until just combined, 30 seconds.

3. In a medium bowl, stir together cinnamon and 2 cups (270 g) of the flour. Gradually add to yeast mixture; beat on low speed until combined, about 1 minute. Gradually add remaining 1½ cups (205 g) flour, beating on low speed until a sticky dough forms, 1 minute. Transfer to a large bowl lightly greased with cooking spray; turn dough to grease top. Cover bowl; refrigerate until dough is thoroughly chilled and firm, at least 4 hours or up to 24 hours.

continued

4 In a medium bowl, place cream cheese, butter, whole milk, vanilla, and remaining ¼ teaspoon salt. Beat with an electric mixer fitted with a paddle attachment on medium speed until smooth, 1 minute. Gradually add powdered sugar, beating until smooth, 1 minute. Spoon glaze into a piping bag or a zip-top plastic bag. Set aside.

5 Turn dough out onto a lightly floured work surface and roll into a 12-inch (30.5-cm) square (about ¼ inch / 6 mm thick). Using a knife or a pizza cutter, cut dough into 2-inch (5-cm) squares. (You should have about 36 pieces.)

6 In a 5 to 6-quart (4.7 to 5.7-L) Dutch oven, pour oil to a depth of 2 inches (5 cm); heat over medium-high heat to 360°F (180°C), adjusting heat as needed to maintain temperature. Working in about 6 batches, carefully add dough pieces to hot oil. Fry until puffy and golden, about 1½ minutes per side.

7 Remove beignets from oil using a slotted spoon; transfer to a wire rack set over a baking sheet. Let stand until just cool enough to handle, 1 to 2 minutes.

8 Snip a 1⁄16 to ⅛-inch (2 to 3-mm) tip off one corner of the filled piping bag. Drizzle glaze over slightly cooled beignets; sprinkle with sanding sugars. Serve immediately.

pavlovas

SERVES 12
ACTIVE: 25 MINUTES
TOTAL: 5 HOURS

1⅓ cups (265 g) granulated sugar

1½ tablespoons cornstarch

6 large egg whites, at room temperature

¼ teaspoon cream of tartar

⅛ teaspoon salt

1½ teaspoons vanilla extract, divided

2 cups (480 ml) cold heavy whipping cream

⅔ cup (165 ml) sour cream

TOPPING SUGGESTIONS:

Lemon Curd (page 34), sliced peaches, fresh berries, mint, basil, or thyme

A pavlova is a type of meringue-based dessert that's crispy and crackly on the outside with a creamy, slightly chewy center. They're normally topped with something creamy and can then be garnished all sorts of ways (a few are suggested below). Unlike rich layer cakes or decadent chocolate delights, they're a light and refreshing alternative to heavy desserts. My first pavlova changed my life—they are seriously that good. Yes, they take time, but I promise they're well worth it.

1 Preheat oven to 225°F (110°C) with racks in upper and lower third positions. Line two large baking sheets with parchment paper. In a small bowl, whisk together sugar and cornstarch; set aside. With an electric mixer fitted with a whisk attachment, beat egg whites on medium-high speed for 1 minute. Add cream of tartar and salt; beat until combined, about 30 seconds. With mixer running on high speed, add sugar mixture 2 tablespoons at a time, beating just until glossy, stiff peaks form and sugar is almost dissolved, about 2 minutes. (Do not overbeat.) Reduce speed to low and beat in ½ teaspoon of the vanilla.

2 Gently spoon about ⅓ cup (75 ml) egg white mixture onto prepared baking sheet in a 3½-inch (9-cm) circle. Repeat with remaining egg white mixture, creating 12 circles total on the two prepared baking sheets, spacing each circle about 1 inch (2.5 cm) apart.

3 Bake in preheated oven until meringues have formed a crust, about 1½ hours, rotating baking sheets between top and bottom racks halfway through bake time.

4 Turn oven off. Let meringues stand in oven with door closed until completely cool with dry and shiny tops, at least 3 hours or up to 10 hours, depending on the humidity of your kitchen. (They should have crisp exteriors and chewy interiors.)

5 Meanwhile, chill bowl of a stand mixer and whisk attachment for 30 minutes. Pour whipping cream into chilled bowl; beat with an electric mixer fitted with the chilled whisk attachment on medium-high speed until soft peaks form, 2 to 3 minutes. Add sour cream and beat until stiff peaks form, about 30 seconds. Beat in remaining 1 teaspoon vanilla until just combined.

6 Arrange meringues on a serving platter and top each with about ¼ cup (60 ml) whipped cream mixture. Garnish pavlovas with desired toppings.

FRAGILE

Masters Party
Fried Chicken Sliders with Pimento Cheese
Southern Sweet Tea Essay
Summer Pasta

Profoto
BASIL

acknowledgments

To my mama, her mama, and all the mama figures in my life—thank you for showing me what true hospitality means; I'm a better woman for it. Rebecca Lang, who gave me my start so many years ago, continues to be a source of inspiration and encouragement- without her I really don't know where I'd be. My producer, Katherine Cobbs, who I could not have done this without, has more hours logged working on this book than I do. She did the hard parts so that I could continue my day job and throughout it all has become a dear friend.

My husband, Luis, along with my parents, Wayne and Sabrina Odom, all cochair my cheering section. Luis is the best recipe taster, dishwasher, and encourager. I'm forever grateful for his patience with my hectic schedule. When you see him, know he's the anchor in this very crazy life of mine. My mama and daddy continue to push me to do anything I set my mind to. I'll never be able to thank them for everything they've done for me.

My incredibly talented colleagues and friends on the *Southern Living* editorial staff have all been constant sources of inspiration and support. I'm especially grateful to Sid Evans and Krissy Tiglias, who are always cheering in my corner. They let me prioritize this book over my other work when things got busy and jumped through multiple hoops to help me get this book off the ground years ago. Betsy Watson was my hotline for cookbook fashion emergencies, and due to her desk's proximity to mine, helped me through the depths of the cookbook trenches.

Daniel Boone offered loads of design input, while Alex Taylor, Brennan Long, and Mary Shannon Hodes all helped in promoting the book, and taking up slack when my normal job duties fell to the wayside. Nellah McGough kept us on budget, and Jeanne Clayton advised on photography and helped coordinate photoshoots. Julia Belagorudsky guided us through the corporate publishing jargon, while Libby Minor and Katherine Polcari polished up my book proposal. Lisa Cericola, Josh Miller, and Kimberly Holland pitched in with ideas and taste-tests. Alana Al-Hatlani did all of that on top of graciously providing notes during layouts. Kelly Hires and Lauren Critelli played a huge role in helping get the word out. They are my PR dynamic duo.

I am forever grateful to Paige Grandjean, my dear friend, former roommate, and favorite person to cook with. Many recipe ideas in this book came from something we've cooked together, and she has been a constant sounding board throughout this multiyear process of publishing a cookbook.

Thanks to my awesome editor, Shawna Mullen, and the entire team at Abrams Books for helping this book live up to its full potential. Designer Danielle Youngsmith created beautiful work that brought my vision to life, and managing editor Krista Keplinger made the copy shine.

The test kitchens at Dotdash Meredith Food Studios are where it all began so many years ago. Vice president Allison Lowery has championed me throughout my journey from test kitchen fellow to cookbook author and helped move mountains to get the recipes tested and photographed. Food studios director Callie Nash went above and beyond to edit recipes, facilitate taste tests, troubleshoot, manage schedules, and so much more. Work-friend-turned- real-friend, Blakeslee Giles, helped make sure we had kitchen and studio space to get our jobs done. Alyson Haynes helped keep recipe testing on schedule, and Tiffany Davis, Renu Dhar, Amanda Holstein, Catherine Jessee, Julia Levy, Craig Ruff, Amanda Stanfield, Giovanna Vazquez, and my dear friend Marianne Williams all made sure my recipes worked and gave suggestions to make them better. Margaret Dickey, Jennifer Wendorf, and Lauren Odum graciously shared their kitchens and allowed us to take over their world throughout our recipe photoshoots. The entire food studios team has had a hand in bringing this book to fruition, and I'm incredibly grateful to them for their encouragement throughout this process.

My dream for a colorful, fun, vibrant, not-too-perfect aesthetic for this book was brought to life by an incredible photography and styling team. Caitlin Bensel brought her magic light to all the recipe images, making studio shots come alive in a way I never dreamed possible. When I saw Lindsey Ellis Beatty's props laid out in her prep space for the first time, I nearly cried tears of joy for how perfectly her style matched mine. I'm forever thankful for Torie Cox, who jumped in from the beginning of this project to help coordinate our dream food team. She makes every piece of food look cover-worthy, and it doesn't hurt that she also loves to yell "Go Dawgs!" My very dear friend Sally McKay claims that all she's good for is washing dishes, but her help on this book goes far beyond that. She styled the cover, helped with wardrobe, and continues to help me get through any life, work, or fashion dilemma that is thrown my way. Robbie Caponetto made my fear of photoshoots disappear and contributed his expert eye. Lydia Pursell made every scene and set feel like real-life, transforming my entire house into something photo-worthy. I'm so glad Priscilla Montiel, who worked a lot on my video sets years ago, was able to come back to my kitchen to make it beautiful one more time. Celine Russell and Louise Robertson made me look and feel my best every day on set. I'm especially grateful for Celine, who went way beyond the call of duty to help with wardrobe and daily encouragement. Nancy Purvis, Rebecca Cummins, Sarah Baurley, Patrick McGough, and Tucker Vines all worked tirelessly behind the scenes to make the sets run smoothly.

To all my former home economics (family and consumer sciences) teachers, advisors and mentors, thank you for giving me knowledge for real life and a passion for sharing my gift with others. The College of Family and Consumer Sciences at the University of Georgia, the Georgia chapter of American Association of Family and Consumer Sciences (GAFCS), and my involvement in Family, Career, and Community Leaders of America (FCCLA) played a huge role in my journey to this career. Now more than ever, it's important to continue to advocate for these programs in schools—it's where students learn practical skills for becoming successful adults.

There are a lot of people who donated props and resources for this book. Lori Ward made the prettiest little layer cakes. Angie Burge from English Village Lane let us use her gorgeous rugs. Gates Shaw lent us his woody Jeep for our tailgate shoot, and Langston Hereford graciously sent her collection of Masters paraphernalia, not once, but twice. Caroline Wilson and Libby Parish from the Tuckernuck Home Collection were extremely generous for sending beautiful accent pieces. The *Southern Living* Collection at Dillard's was also a great resource for styling our sets. This only scratches the surface of all the people who helped bring this book to fruition. For anyone I've missed, please know your contributions mean the world to me. *My Southern Kitchen* has been a huge collaborative effort, and I'm so proud to have been able to work with this roster of talented people. Cheers, y'all!

P.S. I'd be remiss not to thank my dog, Basil, the best kitchen-floor vacuum, wet-nose kisser, and my forever best friend.

about the author

Ivy Odom is the senior lifestyle editor at *Southern Living* and a familiar face of the *Southern Living* brand. She hosted all forty episodes (two seasons) of the syndicated and Emmy-nominated TV show *The Southern Living Show*, and she appears frequently on the *TODAY* show and *Good Morning America*. She is a graduate of the University of Georgia and the culinary arts program at L'Academie de Cuisine in Gaithersburg, Maryland. She lives in Birmingham, Alabama, with her husband, Luis, and her dog, Basil.

index

Page numbers in *italics* indicate recipe photos.

D

E

F

T

V

W

credits

Dotdash Meredith – Southern Living

Editor in Chief: Sid Evans
Associate Group GM: Krissy Tiglias

Produced by Blueline Creative Group LLC

Producer/Editor: Katherine Cobbs

Recipe photography

Photographer: Caitlin Bensel
Prop Stylist: Lindsey Ellis Beatty
Food Stylist: Torie Cox
Food Stylist Assistants: Sally McKay, Rebecca Cummins

Lifestyle photography

Photographer: Robbie Caponetto
Prop Stylist: Lydia Pursell, Prissy Montiel
Prop Stylist Assistants: Tucker Vines, Nancy Purvis
Food Stylists: Torie Cox, Sally McKay
Hair & Makeup: Celine Russell, Louise Robertson
Photo Assistants: Sara Baurley, Patrick McGough

Additional photo credits

Photographs: Ivy Odom: 8, 11, 12, 14 (all except bottom left), 15, 88, 131, 174, 245, 260–261; Art Meripol: 10; Jenna Lindsey: 14 (bottom left), 42; Abby Mims: 15; Victor Protasio: 30, 60, 121, 141, 150, 156, 168, 176, 179, 207, 231, 240, 251, 257; Antonis Achilleos: 55, 87, 184; Greg Dupree: 116, 247; James Ransom: 132; Johnny Autry: 167; Morgan Hunt Glaze: 243; Robbie Caponetto: 235

Food Styling: Telia Johnson: 10; Chelsea Zimmer: 30, 121, 131, 141, 176, 240, 243; Ruth Blackburn: 55, 60, 150, 176, 251; Torie Cox: 87 and 235; Emily Nabors Hall: 116, 156, 231; Julian Hensarling: 132, 247; Rishon Hanners: 168, 179, 257

Prop Styling: Lydia Pursell: 30, 132; Christine Keely: 55, 116, 184; Shelli Royster: 60, 87, 141; Missie Crawford: 116; Christina Brockman: 121; Heather Chadduck Hillegas: 156; Audrey Davis: 168, 179, 207, 231, 257; Christina Daley: 176, 247; Prissy Lee Montiel: 235; Julia Bayless: 240, 243; Ginny Branch: 251

Editor: Shawna Mullen
Designer: Danielle Youngsmith
Managing Editor: Krista Keplinger
Production Manager: Larry Pekarek

Library of Congress Control Number: 2025931673

ISBN: 978-1-4197-7855-1
eISBN: 979-8-88707-507-5

See page 271 for additional photography credits.

Printed and bound in the United States
10 9 8 7 6 5 4

Abrams books are available at special discounts when purchased in quantity for premiums and promotions as well as fundraising or educational use. Special editions can also be created to specification. For details, contact sales@abramsbooks.com or the address below.

ABRAMS The Art of Books
195 Broadway, New York, NY 10007
abramsbooks.com

ABRAMS is represented in the UK and Europe by Abrams & Chronicle Books, 22-24 Ely Place, London EC1N 6TE and Média-Participations, 57 rue Gaston Tessier, 75166 Paris, France.
abramsandchronicle.co.uk and media-participations.com
info@abramsandchronicle.co.uk

Southern Living